MznLnx

Missing Links Exam Preps

Exam Prep for

Management: A Competency-Based Approach

Hellriegel, Jackson, Slocum, 10th Edition

The MznLnx Exam Prep is your link from the texbook and lecture to your exams.
The MznLnx Exam Preps are unauthorized and comprehensive reviews of your textbooks.

MznLnx

Rico
Publications

Exam Prep for Management: A Competency-Based Approach
10th Edition
Hellriegel, Jackson, Slocum

Publisher: Raymond Houge
Assistant Editor: Michael Rouger
Text and Cover Designer: Lisa Buckner
Marketing Manager: Sara Swagger
Project Manager, Editorial Production: Jerry Emerson
Art Director: Vernon Lowerui
Product Manager: Dave Mason
Editorial Assitant: Rachel Guzmanji
Pedagogy: Debra Long
Cover Image: Jim Reed/Getty Images
Text and Cover Printer: City Printing, Inc.
Compositor: Media Mix, Inc.

Printed in the United States
ISBN:

For more information about our products, contact us at:
Dave.Mason@RicoPublications.com

For permission to use material from this text or product, submit a request online to:
Dave.Mason@RicoPublications.com

Contents

TO THE STUDENT

COMPREHENSIVE

The *MznLnx* Exam Prep series is designed to help you pass your exams. Editors at MznLnx review your textbooks and then prepare these practice exams to help you master the textbook material. Unlike study guides, workbooks, and practice tests provided by the texbook publisher and textbook authors, *MznLnx* gives you ***all*** of the material in each chapter in exam form, not just samples, so you can be sure to nail your exam.

MECHANICAL

The MznLnx Exam Prep series creates exams that will help you learn the subject matter as well as test you on your understanding. Each question is designed to help you master the concept. Just working through the exams, you gain an understanding of the subject--its a simple mechanical process that produces success.

INTEGRATED STUDY GUIDE AND REVIEW

MznLnx is not just a set of exams designed to test you, its also a comprehensive review of the subject content. Each exam question is also a review of the concept, making sure that you will get the answer correct without having to go to other sources of material. You learn as you go! Its the easiest way to pass an exam.

HUMOR

Studying can be tedious and dry. MznLnx's instructional design includes moderate humor within the exam questions on occassion, to break the tedium and revitalize the brain

1. _________ for short is a descriptive term for certain executives in a business operation. It is also a formal title held by some business executives, most commonly in the hospitality industry.

A _________ has broad, overall responsibility for a business or organization. Whereas a manager may be responsible for one functional area, the _________ is responsible for all areas.

a. Chief technology officer
b. Chief knowledge officer
c. Managing director
d. General manager

2. A _________ is a list of the general tasks and responsibilities of a position. Typically, it also includes to whom the position reports, specifications such as the qualifications needed by the person in the job, salary range for the position, etc. A _________ is usually developed by conducting a job analysis, which includes examining the tasks and sequences of tasks necessary to perform the job.

a. Recruitment Process Insourcing
b. Recruitment
c. Recruitment advertising
d. Job description

3. The _________ is a United States labor law allowing an employee to take unpaid leave due to a serious health condition that makes the employee unable to perform his job or to care for a sick family member or to care for a new son or daughter (including by birth, adoption or foster care.) The bill was among the first signed into law by President Bill Clinton in his first term.

a. Contributory negligence
b. Family and Medical Leave Act of 1993
c. Harvester Judgment
d. Sarbanes-Oxley Act of 2002

1. _________ is a form of leadership in which the authority of an organization or a ruling regime is largely tied to tradition or custom. The main reason for the given state of affairs is that it 'has always been that way'.

In sociology, the concept of _________ comes from Max Weber's tripartite classification of authority, the other two forms being charismatic authority and rational-legal authority.

a. 28-hour day
b. Rational-legal authority
c. Traditional authority
d. 1990 Clean Air Act

2. The sociologist Max Weber defined _________ as 'resting on devotion to the exceptional sanctity, heroism or exemplary character of an individual person, and of the normative patterns or order revealed or ordained by him.' _________ is one of three forms of authority laid out in Weber's tripartite classification of authority, the other two being traditional authority and rational-legal authority. The concept has acquired wide usage among sociologists.

In his writings about _________, Weber applies the term charisma to 'a certain quality of an individual personality, by virtue of which he is set apart from ordinary men and treated as endowed with supernatural, superhuman, or at least specifically exceptional powers or qualities.

a. 28-hour day
b. 1990 Clean Air Act
c. Charismatic authority
d. Rational-legal authority

3. _________ is a form of leadership in which the authority of an organization or a ruling regime is largely tied to legal rationality, legal legitimacy and bureaucracy. The majority of the modern states of the twentieth century are rational-legal authorities, according to those who use this form of classification.

In sociology, the concept of rational-legal domination comes from Max Weber's tripartite classification of authority; the other two forms being traditional authority and charismatic authority.

a. 28-hour day
b. Traditional authority
c. 1990 Clean Air Act
d. Rational-legal authority

4. _________ is a term defined by the Oxford English Dictionary as an individual's 'course or progress through life '. It is usually considered to pertain to remunerative work (and sometimes also formal education.)

The etymology of the term is somewhat ironic in that it comes from the Latin word carrera, which means race .

a. Career
b. Career planning
c. Nursing shortage
d. Spatial mismatch

5. In economics, business, retail, and accounting, a _________ is the value of money that has been used up to produce something, and hence is not available for use anymore. In economics, a _________ is an alternative that is given up as a result of a decision. In business, the _________ may be one of acquisition, in which case the amount of money expended to acquire it is counted as _________.
a. Fixed costs
b. Cost allocation
c. Cost
d. Cost overrun

6. _________ is a theory of management that analyzes and synthesizes workflows, with the objective of improving labour productivity. The core ideas of the theory were developed by Frederick Winslow Taylor in the 1880s and 1890s, and were first published in his monographs, Shop Management and The Principles of _________ Taylor believed that decisions based upon tradition and rules of thumb should be replaced by precise procedures developed after careful study of an individual at work.
a. Master production schedule
b. Capacity planning
c. Scientific management
d. Value engineering

7. A _________ is a type of bar chart that illustrates a project schedule. _________s illustrate the start and finish dates of the terminal elements and summary elements of a project. Terminal elements and summary elements comprise the work breakdown structure of the project.
a. 28-hour day
b. 33 Strategies of War
c. 1990 Clean Air Act
d. Gantt chart

8. The _________ is a standardized, on-scene, all-hazard incident management concept. It is a management protocol originally designed for emergency management agencies in the United States which was later federalized there. It has since been adopted by agencies in other countries.

a. Incident Command Structure
b. AAAI
c. A4e
d. A Stake in the Outcome

9. The _________ is a form of reactivity whereby subjects improve an aspect of their behavior being experimentally measured simply in response to the fact that they are being studied, not in response to any particular experimental manipulation.

The term was coined in 1955 by Henry A. Landsberger when analyzing older experiments from 1924-1932 at the Hawthorne Works (outside Chicago.) Hawthorne Works had commissioned a study to see if its workers would become more productive in higher or lower levels of light.

a. 33 Strategies of War
b. 1990 Clean Air Act
c. 28-hour day
d. Hawthorne effect

10. _________ describes the situation when output from (or information about the result of) an event or phenomenon in the past will influence the same event/phenomenon in the present or future. When an event is part of a chain of cause-and-effect that forms a circuit or loop, then the event is said to 'feed back' into itself.

_________ is also a synonym for:

- _________ signal; the information about the initial event that is the basis for subsequent modification of the event.
- _________ loop; the causal path that leads from the initial generation of the _________ signal to the subsequent modification of the event.

_________ is a mechanism, process or signal that is looped back to control a system within itself. Such a loop is called a _________ loop.

a. Feedback
b. Positive feedback
c. Feedback loop
d. 1990 Clean Air Act

11. _________ is an effective method of monitoring a process through the use of control charts. Control charts enable the use of objective criteria for distinguishing background variation from events of significance based on statistical techniques. Much of its power lies in the ability to monitor both process center and its variation about that center.

a. Process capability
b. Single Minute Exchange of Die
c. Quality control
d. Statistical process control

12. _________ is a business management strategy aimed at embedding awareness of quality in all organizational processes. _________ has been widely used in manufacturing, education, hospitals, call centers, government, and service industries, as well as NASA space and science programs.

As defined by the International Organization for Standardization (ISO):

> '_________ is a management approach for an organization, centered on quality, based on the participation of all its members and aiming at long-term success through customer satisfaction, and benefits to all members of the organization and to society.' ISO 8402:1994

One major aim is to reduce variation from every process so that greater consistency of effort is obtained. (Royse, D., Thyer, B., Padgett D., ' Logan T., 2006)

a. 1990 Clean Air Act
b. Quality management
c. 28-hour day
d. Total quality management

13. _________ is one of the managerial functions like planning, organizing, staffing and directing. It is an important function because it helps to check the errors and to take the corrective action so that deviation from standards are minimized and stated goals of the organization are achieved in desired manner.According to modern concepts, _________ is a foreseeing action whereas earlier concept of _________ was used only when errors were detected. _________ in management means setting standards, measuring actual performance and taking corrective action.

a. Control
b. Turnover
c. Schedule of reinforcement
d. Decision tree pruning

14. In engineering and manufacturing, _________ and quality engineering are used in developing systems to ensure products or services are designed and produced to meet or exceed customer requirements. Refer to the definition by Merriam-Webster for further information . These systems are often developed in conjunction with other business and engineering disciplines using a cross-functional approach.

a. Quality control
b. Single Minute Exchange of Die
c. Process capability
d. Statistical process control

15. _________ can be considered to have three main components: quality control, quality assurance and quality improvement. _________ is focused not only on product quality, but also the means to achieve it. _________ therefore uses quality assurance and control of processes as well as products to achieve more consistent quality.
a. 28-hour day
b. 1990 Clean Air Act
c. Total quality management
d. Quality management

16. A _________ is a research instrument consisting of a series of questions and other prompts for the purpose of gathering information from respondents. Although they are often designed for statistical analysis of the responses, this is not always the case. The _________ was invented by Sir Francis Galton.
a. Questionnaire construction
b. Mystery shoppers
c. Questionnaire
d. Structured interview

1. _________ comprises a range of practices used in an organisation to identify, create, represent, distribute and enable adoption of insights and experiences. Such insights and experiences comprise knowledge, either embodied in individuals or embedded in organisational processes or practice.

An established discipline since 1991 , _________ includes courses taught in the fields of business administration, information systems, management, and library and information sciences .

a. 28-hour day
b. Knowledge management
c. 33 Strategies of War
d. 1990 Clean Air Act

2. The _________ of 1990 (ADA) is the short title of United States (Pub.L. 101-336, 104 Stat. 327, enacted July 26, 1990), codified at 42 U.S.C. Â§ 12101 et seq. It was signed into law on July 26, 1990, by President George H. W. Bush, and later amended with changes effective January 1, 2009. The ADA is a wide-ranging civil rights law that prohibits, under certain circumstances, discrimination based on disability. It affords similar protections against discrimination to Americans with disabilities as the Civil Rights Act of 1964,

a. Employment discrimination
b. Equal Pay Act of 1963
c. Australian labour law
d. Americans with Disabilities Act

3. _________ or _________ data refers to selected population characteristics as used in government, marketing or opinion research, or the _________ profiles used in such research. Note the distinction from the term 'demography' Commonly-used _________s include race, age, income, disabilities, mobility (in terms of travel time to work or number of vehicles available), educational attainment, home ownership, employment status, and even location.

a. Abraham Harold Maslow
b. Affiliation
c. Adam Smith
d. Demographic

4. A _________ is a set of consistent ethic values (more specifically the personal and cultural values) and measures used for the purpose of ethical or ideological integrity. A well defined _________ is a moral code.

Fred Wenst>øp and Arild Myrmel have proposed a structure for corporate _________s that consists of three value categories. These are considered complementary and juxtaposed on the same level if illustrated graphically on for instance an organization's web page. The first value category is Core Values, which prescribe the attitude and character of an organization, and are often found in sections on Code of conduct on its web page. The philosophical antecedents of these values are Virtue ethics, which is often attributed to Aristotle. Protected Values are protected through rules, standards and certifications. They are often concerned with areas such as health, environment and safety. The third category, Created Values, is the values that stakeholders, including the shareholders expect in return for their contributions to the firm. These values are subject to trade-off by decision-makers or bargaining processes. This process is explained further in Stakeholder theory.

a. Value system
b. 33 Strategies of War
c. 1990 Clean Air Act
d. 28-hour day

5. _________ is a term used to describe any moral, political that stresses human interdependence and the importance of a collective, rather than the importance of separate individuals. Collectivists focus on community and society, and seek to give priority to group goals over individual goals. The philosophical underpinnings of _________ are for some related to holism or organicism - the view that the whole is greater than the sum of its parts/pieces.

a. Collaborative methods
b. 1990 Clean Air Act
c. 28-hour day
d. Collectivism

6. The _________ is a bank regulation, which sets a framework on how banks and depository institutions must handle their capital. The categorization of assets and capital is highly standardized so that it can be risk weighted. Internationally, the Basel Committee on Banking Supervision housed at the Bank for International Settlements influence each country's banking _________s.

a. 1990 Clean Air Act
b. Lock box
c. Reserve requirement
d. Capital requirement

7. _________, in microeconomics, are the cost advantages that a business obtains due to expansion. They are factors that cause a producer's average cost per unit to fall as scale is increased. _________ is a long run concept and refers to reductions in unit cost as the size of a facility, or scale, increases.

a. Economies of scope
b. A Stake in the Outcome
c. Economies of scale
d. A4e

8. In marketing, _________ is the process of distinguishing the differences of a product or offering from others, to make it more attractive to a particular target market. This involves differentiating it from competitors' products as well as one's own product offerings.
a. Market share
b. PEST analysis
c. Market development
d. Product differentiation

9. _________ is an advertisement in which a particular product specifically mentions a competitor by name for the express purpose of showing why the competitor is inferior to the product naming it.

This should not be confused with parody advertisements, where a fictional product is being advertised for the purpose of poking fun at the particular advertisement, nor should it be confused with the use of a coined brand name for the purpose of comparing the product without actually naming an actual competitor. ('Wikipedia tastes better and is less filling than the Encyclopedia Galactica.')

In the 1980s, during what has been referred to as the cola wars, soft-drink manufacturer Pepsi ran a series of advertisements where people, caught on hidden camera, in a blind taste test, chose Pepsi over rival Coca-Cola.

a. 33 Strategies of War
b. 1990 Clean Air Act
c. Comparative advertising
d. 28-hour day

10. The _________ of 1968 is a United States federal law designed to protect consumers in credit transactions, by requiring clear disclosure of key terms of the lending arrangement and all costs. The statute is contained in Title I of the Consumer Credit Protection Act, as amended (15 U.S.C. Â§ 1601 et seq.).
a. Truth in Lending Act
b. 1990 Clean Air Act
c. Fair Credit Reporting Act
d. 28-hour day

11. A _________ is an entity formed between two or more parties to undertake economic activity together. The parties agree to create a new entity by both contributing equity, and they then share in the revenues, expenses, and control of the enterprise. The venture can be for one specific project only, or a continuing business relationship such as the Fuji Xerox _________.

a. Joint venture
b. Civil Rights Act of 1991
c. Meritor Savings Bank v. Vinson
d. Patent

12. An _________ is a person who has possession of an enterprise and assumes significant accountability for the inherent risks and the outcome. It is an ambitious leader who combines land, labor, and capital to create and market new goods or services. The term is a loanword from French and was first defined by the Irish economist Richard Cantillon.

a. A4e
b. A Stake in the Outcome
c. AAAI
d. Entrepreneur

13. _________ is one of the four elements of marketing mix. An organization or set of organizations (go-betweens) involved in the process of making a product or service available for use or consumption by a consumer or business user.

The other three parts of the marketing mix are product, pricing, and promotion.

a. Matching theory
b. Distribution
c. Job creation programs
d. Missing completely at random

1. _________ is the branch of economics that studies the dynamics of exchange rates, foreign investment, and how these affect international trade. It also studies international projects, international investments and capital flows, and trade deficits. It includes the study of futures, options and currency swaps.
   a. A Stake in the Outcome
   b. International finance
   c. AAAI
   d. A4e

2. A _________ is an entity formed between two or more parties to undertake economic activity together. The parties agree to create a new entity by both contributing equity, and they then share in the revenues, expenses, and control of the enterprise. The venture can be for one specific project only, or a continuing business relationship such as the Fuji Xerox _________.
   a. Patent
   b. Meritor Savings Bank v. Vinson
   c. Civil Rights Act of 1991
   d. Joint venture

3. A _________ is a type of business entity in which partners (owners) share with each other the profits or losses of the business. _________s are often favored over corporations for taxation purposes, as the _________ structure does not generally incur a tax on profits before it is distributed to the partners (i.e. there is no dividend tax levied.) However, depending on the _________ structure and the jurisdiction in which it operates, owners of a _________ may be exposed to greater personal liability than they would as shareholders of a corporation.
   a. Partnership
   b. Mediation
   c. Federal Employers Liability Act
   d. Due process

4. _________ is the incidence or process of transferring ownership of a business, enterprise, agency or public service from the public sector (government) to the private sector (business.) In a broader sense, _________ refers to transfer of any government function to the private sector including governmental functions like revenue collection and law enforcement.
   a. 1990 Clean Air Act
   b. Privatization
   c. 28-hour day
   d. Performance reports

5. An _________ is an organization founded and funded by businesses that operate in a specific industry. An industry trade association participates in public relations activities such as advertising, education, political donations, lobbying and publishing, but its main focus is collaboration between companies, or standardization. Associations may offer other services, such as producing conferences, networking or charitable events or offering classes or educational materials.

a. AAAI
b. A4e
c. A Stake in the Outcome
d. Industry trade group

6. An _________ is a person who has possession of an enterprise and assumes significant accountability for the inherent risks and the outcome. It is an ambitious leader who combines land, labor, and capital to create and market new goods or services. The term is a loanword from French and was first defined by the Irish economist Richard Cantillon.

a. AAAI
b. Entrepreneur
c. A Stake in the Outcome
d. A4e

7. In decision theory and estimation theory, the _________ of an estimator, $\hat{\theta}$, of an unknown parameter of the distribution, θ, is the expected value of the loss function

$$R(\theta, \hat{\theta}) = \mathbb{E}_\theta L(\theta, \hat{\theta}) = \int L(\theta, \hat{\theta})\, dP_\theta.$$

where dP_θ is a probability measure parametrized by θ.

- For a scalar parameter θ and a quadratic loss function,

  $$L(\theta, \hat{\theta}) = (\theta - \hat{\theta})^2$$

  the _________ function becomes the mean squared error of the estimate,

  $$R(\theta, \hat{\theta}) = E_\theta(\theta - \hat{\theta})^2$$

- In density estimation, the unknown parameter is probability density itself. The loss function is typically chosen to be a norm in an appropriate function space. For example, for L^2 norm,

  $$L(f, \hat{f}) = \|f - \hat{f}\|_2^2$$

  the _________ function becomes the mean integrated squared error

  $$R(f, \hat{f}) = E\|f - \hat{f}\|^2$$

.

a. Risk aversion
b. Risk
c. Linear model
d. Financial modeling

8. A _________ is a formal (explicit) agreement among firms. It is a formal organization of producers that agree to coordinate prices and production. _________s usually occur in an oligopolistic industry, where there is a small number of sellers and usually involve homogeneous products.

a. 1990 Clean Air Act
b. 28-hour day
c. 33 Strategies of War
d. Cartel

9. _________ is a type of trade policy that allows traders to act and transact without interference from government. Thus, the policy permits trading partners mutual gains from trade, with goods and services produced according to the theory of comparative advantage.

Under a _________ policy, prices are a reflection of true supply and demand, and are the sole determinant of resource allocation.

a. 1990 Clean Air Act
b. 28-hour day
c. 33 Strategies of War
d. Free Trade

10. _________ is a designated group of countries that have agreed to eliminate tariffs, quotas and preferences on most (if not all) goods and services traded between them. It can be considered the second stage of economic integration. Countries choose this kind of economic integration form if their economical structures are complementary.

a. 1990 Clean Air Act
b. 28-hour day
c. Free trade area
d. 33 Strategies of War

11. The _________ was the outcome of the failure of negotiating governments to create the International Trade Organization (ITO.) GATT was formed in 1947 and lasted until 1994, when it was replaced by the World Trade Organization. The Bretton Woods Conference had introduced the idea for an organization to regulate trade as part of a larger plan for economic recovery after World War II.

a. 1990 Clean Air Act
b. 28-hour day
c. Multilateral treaty
d. General Agreement on Tariffs and Trade

12. The _________ is a trilateral trade bloc in North America created by the governments of the United States, Canada, and Mexico. The agreement creating the trade bloc came into force on January 1, 1994. It superseded the Canada-United States Free Trade Agreement between the U.S. and Canada.

a. Career portfolios
b. Trade union
c. Business war game
d. North American Free Trade Agreement

13. _________ are legal property rights over creations of the mind, both artistic and commercial, and the corresponding fields of law. Under _________ law, owners are granted certain exclusive rights to a variety of intangible assets, such as musical, literary, and artistic works; ideas, discoveries and inventions; and words, phrases, symbols, and designs. Common types of _________ include copyrights, trademarks, patents, industrial design rights and trade secrets.

a. Intent
b. Unemployment Action Center
c. Equal Pay Act
d. Intellectual property

14. A _________ is a set of exclusive rights granted by a state to an inventor or his assignee for a limited period of time in exchange for a disclosure of an invention.

The procedure for granting _________s, the requirements placed on the _________ee and the extent of the exclusive rights vary widely between countries according to national laws and international agreements. Typically, however, a _________ application must include one or more claims defining the invention which must be new, inventive, and useful or industrially applicable.

a. Federal Trade Commission Act
b. Labor Management Reporting and Disclosure Act
c. Food, Drug, and Cosmetic Act
d. Patent

15. A _________ is a distinctive sign or indicator used by an individual, business organization, or other legal entity to identify that the products and/or services to consumers with which the _________ appears originate from a unique source and to distinguish its products or services from those of other entities.
a. Succession planning
b. Virtual team
c. Kanban
d. Trademark

16. _________ plant, and equipment, is a term used in accountancy for assets and property which cannot easily be converted into cash. This can be compared with current assets such as cash or bank accounts, which are described as liquid assets. In most cases, only tangible assets are referred to as fixed.
a. 28-hour day
b. 33 Strategies of War
c. 1990 Clean Air Act
d. Fixed asset

17. A _________ or maquila is a factory that imports materials and equipment on a duty-free and tariff-free basis for assembly or manufacturing and then re-exports the assembled product, usually back to the originating country. A maquila is also referred to as a 'twin plant', or 'in-bond' industry. Nearly half a million Mexicans are employed in _________s.

a. Maquiladora
b. 28-hour day
c. 1990 Clean Air Act
d. 33 Strategies of War

18. _________ refers to the aggregated strategies of single business firm or a strategic business unit (SBU) in a diversified corporation. According to Michael Porter, a firm must formulate a _________ that incorporates either cost leadership, differentiation or focus in order to achieve a sustainable competitive advantage and long-term success in its chosen arenas or industries.

Functional strategies include marketing strategies, new product development strategies, human resource strategies, financial strategies, legal strategies, supply-chain strategies, and information technology management strategies.

a. Switching cost
b. Strategic thinking
c. Competitive heterogeneity
d. Business Strategy

19. _________ is exchange of capital, goods, and services across international borders or territories. In most countries, it represents a significant share of gross domestic product (GDP.) While _________ has been present throughout much of history , its economic, social, and political importance has been on the rise in recent centuries.

a. A4e
b. A Stake in the Outcome
c. International trade
d. AAAI

20. _________ is exchanging goods or services that are paid for, in whole or part, with other goods or services.

There are five main variants of _________:

- Barter: Exchange of goods or services directly for other goods or services without the use of money as means of purchase or payment.
- Switch trading: Practice in which one company sells to another its obligation to make a purchase in a given country.
- Counter purchase: Sale of goods and services to a country by a company that promises to make a future purchase of a specific product from the country.
- Buyback: occurs when a firm builds a plant in a country - or supplies technology, equipment, training, or other services to the country and agrees to take a certain percentage of the plant's output as partial payment for the contract.
- Offset: Agreement that a company will offset a hard - currency purchase of an unspecified product from that nation in the future. Agreement by one nation to buy a product from another, subject to the purchase of some or all of the components and raw materials from the buyer of the finished product, or the assembly of such product in the buyer nation.

_________ also occurs when countries lack sufficient hard currency, or when other types of market trade are impossible85 a barrel while Iraq oil sales into Asia were valued at about $22 a barrel. In 2001, India agreed to swap 1.5 million tonnes of Iraqi crude under the oil-for-food program.

a. Trade credit
b. Buy-sell agreement
c. 1990 Clean Air Act
d. Countertrade

21. _________ refers to the methods of practicing and using another person's business philosophy. The franchisor grants the independent operator the right to distribute its products, techniques, and trademarks for a percentage of gross monthly sales and a royalty fee. Various tangibles and intangibles such as national or international advertising, training, and other support services are commonly made available by the franchisor.
a. Franchising
b. 28-hour day
c. ServiceMaster
d. 1990 Clean Air Act

22. A _________ is a formal relationship between two or more parties to pursue a set of agreed upon goals or to meet a critical business need while remaining independent organizations.

Partners may provide the _________ with resources such as products, distribution channels, manufacturing capability, project funding, capital equipment, knowledge, expertise, or intellectual property. The alliance is a cooperation or collaboration which aims for a synergy where each partner hopes that the benefits from the alliance will be greater than those from individual efforts.

a. Process automation
b. Golden parachute
c. Farmshoring
d. Strategic Alliance

23. _________ as defined in business terms is an organization's strategic guide to globalization. A sound _________ should address these questions: what must be (versus what is) the extent of market presence in the world's major markets? How to build the necessary global presence? What must be (versus what is) the optimal locations around the world for the various value chain activities? How to run global presence into global competitive advantage?

Academic research on _________ came of age during the 1980s, including work by Michael Porter and Christopher Bartlett ' Sumantra Ghoshal. Among the forces perceived to bring about the globalization of competition were convergence in economic systems and technological change, especially in information technology, that facilitated and required the coordination of a multinational firm's strategy on a worldwide scale.

a. 33 Strategies of War
b. 28-hour day
c. 1990 Clean Air Act
d. Global strategy

24. _________s are parts of a corporation that directly add to its profit.

A _________ manager is held accountable for both revenues, and costs (expenses), and therefore, profits. What this means in terms of managerial responsibilities is that the manager has to drive the sales revenue generating activities which leads to cash inflows and at the same time control the cost (cash outflows) causing activities.

a. Factory overhead
b. Customer profitability
c. Process costing
d. Profit center

25. A _________ is a research instrument consisting of a series of questions and other prompts for the purpose of gathering information from respondents. Although they are often designed for statistical analysis of the responses, this is not always the case. The _________ was invented by Sir Francis Galton.

a. Questionnaire construction

b. Structured interview

c. Mystery shoppers

d. Questionnaire

1. _________ according to Onuoha (2007) is the practice of starting new organizations or revitalizing mature organizations, particularly new businesses generally in response to identified opportunities. _________ is often a difficult undertaking, as a vast majority of new businesses fail. Entrepreneurial activities are substantially different depending on the type of organization that is being started.

a. A Stake in the Outcome
b. A4e
c. AAAI
d. Entrepreneurship

2. An _________ is a person who has possession of an enterprise and assumes significant accountability for the inherent risks and the outcome. It is an ambitious leader who combines land, labor, and capital to create and market new goods or services. The term is a loanword from French and was first defined by the Irish economist Richard Cantillon.

a. A4e
b. A Stake in the Outcome
c. AAAI
d. Entrepreneur

3. _________, commonly referred to as 'eBusiness' or 'e-Business', may be defined as the utilization of information and communication technologies (ICT) in support of all the activities of business. Commerce constitutes the exchange of products and services between businesses, groups and individuals and hence can be seen as one of the essential activities of any business. Hence, electronic commerce or eCommerce focuses on the use of ICT to enable the external activities and relationships of the business with individuals, groups and other businesses .

a. A4e
b. Electronic business
c. A Stake in the Outcome
d. AAAI

4. _________ are programs designed to accelerate the successful development of entrepreneurial companies through an array of business support resources and services, developed and orchestrated by incubator management and offered both in the incubator and through its network of contacts. Incubators vary in the way they deliver their services, in their organizational structure, and in the types of clients they serve. Successful completion of a business incubation program increases the likelihood that a start-up company will stay in business for the long term: Historically, 87% of incubator graduates stay in business.

a. 33 Strategies of War
b. 1990 Clean Air Act
c. Business incubators
d. 28-hour day

5. A _________ is a business that is privately owned and operated, with a small number of employees and relatively low volume of sales. The legal definition of 'small' often varies by country and industry, but is generally under 100 employees in the United States and under 50 employees in the European Union. In comparison, the definition of mid-sized business by the number of employees is generally under 500 in the U.S. and 250 for the European Union.

a. Pre-determined overhead rate
b. Critical Success Factor
c. Golden Boot Compensation
d. Small Business

6. A _________ is a formal statement of a set of business goals, the reasons why they are believed attainable, and the plan for reaching those goals. It may also contain background information about the organization or team attempting to reach those goals.

The business goals may be defined for for-profit or for non-profit organizations.

a. Time management
b. Crisis management
c. Distributed management
d. Business plan

7. A _________ is a person or investment firm that makes venture investments, and these _________s are expected to bring managerial and technical expertise as well as capital to their investments. A venture capital fund refers to a pooled investment vehicle that primarily invests the financial capital of third-party investors in enterprises that are too risky for the standard capital markets or bank loans.

Venture capital is also associated with job creation, the knowledge economy and used as a proxy measure of innovation within an economic sector or geography.

a. Private equity
b. Limited liability corporation
c. Venture capitalist
d. Limited partners

8. _________ is the branch of economics that studies the dynamics of exchange rates, foreign investment, and how these affect international trade. It also studies international projects, international investments and capital flows, and trade deficits. It includes the study of futures, options and currency swaps.

a. AAAI
b. A Stake in the Outcome
c. A4e
d. International finance

9. A _________ is a body of elected or appointed members who jointly oversee the activities of a company or organization. The body sometimes has a different name, such as board of trustees, board of governors, board of managers, or executive board. It is often simply referred to as 'the board.'

A board's activities are determined by the powers, duties, and responsibilities delegated to it or conferred on it by an authority outside itself.

a. Competition law
b. Foreign Corrupt Practices Act
c. Clean Water Act
d. Board of directors

10. _________ is the practice of using entrepreneurial skills without taking on the risks or accountability associated with entrepreneurial activities. It is practiced by employees within an established organization using a business model. Employees, perhaps engaged in a special project within a larger firm are supposed to behave as entrepreneurs, even though they have the resources and capabilities of the larger firm to draw upon.
a. A4e
b. Intrapreneurship
c. AAAI
d. A Stake in the Outcome

1. _________ is a contract between two parties, one being the employer and the other being the employee. An employee may be defined as: 'A person in the service of another under any contract of hire, express or implied, oral or written, where the employer has the power or right to control and direct the employee in the material details of how the work is to be performed.' Black's Law Dictionary page 471 (5th ed. 1979.)

a. Exit interview
b. Employment rate
c. Employment counsellor
d. Employment

2. The term _________ was created by President Lyndon B. Johnson when he signed Executive Order 11246 on September 24, 1965, created to prohibit federal contractors from discriminating against employees on the basis of race, sex, creed, religion, color, or national origin. In more recent times, most employers have also added sexual orientation to the list of non-discrimination.

The Executive Order also required contractors to implement affirmative action plans to increase the participation of minorities and women in the workplace.

a. AAAI
b. Equal Employment Opportunity
c. A4e
d. A Stake in the Outcome

3. The _________ of 2002 (Pub.L. 107-204, 116 Stat. 745, enacted July 30, 2002), also known as the Public Company Accounting Reform and Investor Protection Act of 2002 and commonly called Sarbanes-Oxley, Sarbox or SOX, is a United States federal law enacted on July 30, 2002, as a reaction to a number of major corporate and accounting scandals including those affecting Enron, Tyco International, Adelphia, Peregrine Systems and WorldCom.

a. Sarbanes-Oxley Act of 2002
b. Fair Labor Standards Act
c. Letter of credit
d. Sarbanes-Oxley Act

4. A _________ is a person who alleges misconduct. More complex definitions may be used, but the issue is that the _________ usually faces reprisal. The misconduct may be classified in many ways; for example, a violation of a law, rule, regulation and/or a direct threat to public interest, such as fraud, health/safety violations, and corruption.

a. 28-hour day
b. 1990 Clean Air Act
c. 33 Strategies of War
d. Whistleblower

5. A _________ is a research instrument consisting of a series of questions and other prompts for the purpose of gathering information from respondents. Although they are often designed for statistical analysis of the responses, this is not always the case. The _________ was invented by Sir Francis Galton.

a. Structured interview
b. Questionnaire
c. Questionnaire construction
d. Mystery shoppers

6. _________ is Latin for 'Let the buyer beware'. Generally _________ is the property law doctrine that controls the sale of real property after the date of closing.

Under the doctrine of _________, the buyer could not recover from the seller for defects on the property that rendered the property unfit for ordinary purposes. The only exception was if the seller actively concealed latent defects. The modern trend in the US, however, is one of the Implied Warranty of Fitness that applies only to the sale of new residential housing by a builder-seller and the rule of _________ applies to all other sale situations.

a. 1990 Clean Air Act
b. 28-hour day
c. 33 Strategies of War
d. Caveat emptor

7. The _________ 1970 is an Act of the United Kingdom Parliament which prohibits any less favourable treatment between men and women in terms of pay and conditions of employment. It came into force on 29 December 1975. The term pay is interpreted in a broad sense to include, on top of wages, things like holidays, pension rights, company perks and some kinds of bonuses.

a. Australian labour law
b. Architectural Barriers Act of 1968
c. Oncale v. Sundowner Offshore Services
d. Equal Pay Act

8. _________ is a pattern of resource use that aims to meet human needs while preserving the environment so that these needs can be met not only in the present, but also for future generations. The term was used by the Brundtland Commission which coined what has become the most often-quoted definition of _________ as development that 'meets the needs of the present without compromising the ability of future generations to meet their own needs.'

_________ ties together concern for the carrying capacity of natural systems with the social challenges facing humanity. As early as the 1970s 'sustainability' was employed to describe an economy 'in equilibrium with basic ecological support systems.' Ecologists have pointed to the 'limits of growth' and presented the alternative of a 'steady state economy' in order to address environmental concerns.

a. Sustainable development
b. Sustainable business
c. Sustainability reporting
d. Global Reporting Initiative

9. The general definition of an _________ is an evaluation of a person, organization, system, process, project or product. _________s are performed to ascertain the validity and reliability of information; also to provide an assessment of a system's internal control. The goal of an _________ is to express an opinion on the person / organization/system (etc) in question, under evaluation based on work done on a test basis.

a. A Stake in the Outcome
b. Audit
c. Internal control
d. Audit committee

1. _________ is an organization's process of defining its strategy and making decisions on allocating its resources to pursue this strategy, including its capital and people. Various business analysis techniques can be used in _________, including SWOT analysis (Strengths, Weaknesses, Opportunities, and Threats) and PEST analysis (Political, Economic, Social, and Technological analysis) or STEER analysis involving Socio-cultural, Technological, Economic, Ecological, and Regulatory factors and EPISTEL (Environment, Political, Informatic, Social, Technological, Economic and Legal)

_________ is the formal consideration of an organization's future course. All _________ deals with at least one of three key questions:

1. 'What do we do?'
2. 'For whom do we do it?'
3. 'How do we excel?'

In business _________, the third question is better phrased 'How can we beat or avoid competition?'. (Bradford and Duncan, page 1.)

a. 28-hour day
b. 33 Strategies of War
c. 1990 Clean Air Act
d. Strategic planning

2. The 'business case for _________', theorizes that in a global marketplace, a company that employs a diverse workforce (both men and women, people of many generations, people from ethnically and racially diverse backgrounds etc.) is better able to understand the demographics of the marketplace it serves and is thus better equipped to thrive in that marketplace than a company that has a more limited range of employee demographics.

An additional corollary suggests that a company that supports the _________ of its workforce can also improve employee satisfaction, productivity and retention.

a. Diversity
b. Trademark
c. Virtual team
d. Kanban

3. _________ is used to assign the available resources in an economic way. It is part of resource management.

In strategic planning,is a plan for using available resources, for example human resources, especially in the near term, to achieve goals for the future.

a. 33 Strategies of War
b. 1990 Clean Air Act
c. 28-hour day
d. Resource allocation

4. A _________ is a process in which a potential employee is evaluated by an employer for prospective employment in their company, organization and was established in the late 16th century.

A _________ typically precedes the hiring decision, and is used to evaluate the candidate. The interview is usually preceded by the evaluation of submitted résumés from interested candidates, then selecting a small number of candidates for interviews.

a. Split shift
b. Payrolling
c. Supported employment
d. Job interview

5. The _________ of 2002 (Pub.L. 107-204, 116 Stat. 745, enacted July 30, 2002), also known as the Public Company Accounting Reform and Investor Protection Act of 2002 and commonly called Sarbanes-Oxley, Sarbox or SOX, is a United States federal law enacted on July 30, 2002, as a reaction to a number of major corporate and accounting scandals including those affecting Enron, Tyco International, Adelphia, Peregrine Systems and WorldCom.

a. Fair Labor Standards Act
b. Letter of credit
c. Sarbanes-Oxley Act of 2002
d. Sarbanes-Oxley Act

6. _________ is understood as a business unit within the overall corporate identity which is distinguishable from other business because it serves a defined external market where management can conduct strategic planning in relation to products and markets. When companies become really large, they are best thought of as being composed of a number of businesses (or _________s.)

In the broader domain of strategic management, the phrase '_________' came into use in the 1960s, largely as a result of General Electric's many units.

a. Switching cost
b. Strategic business unit
c. Strategic drift
d. Strategic group

7. In microeconomics and strategic management, the term _________ describes a type of ownership and control. It is a strategy used by a business or corporation that seeks to sell a type of product in numerous markets. _________ in marketing is much more common than vertical integration is in production.

a. No-bid contract
b. Horizontal integration
c. Career development
d. Farmshoring

8. _________ is an integrated communications-based process through which individuals and communities discover that existing and newly-identified needs and wants may be satisfied by the products and services of others.

_________ is defined by the American _________ Association as the activity, set of institutions, and processes for creating, communicating, delivering, and exchanging offerings that have value for customers, clients, partners, and society at large. The term developed from the original meaning which referred literally to going to market, as in shopping, or going to a market to buy or sell goods or services.

a. Marketing
b. Disruptive technology
c. Customer relationship management
d. Market development

9. A _________ is a process that can allow an organization to concentrate its limited resources on the greatest opportunities to increase sales and achieve a sustainable competitive advantage. A _________ should be centered around the key concept that customer satisfaction is the main goal.

A _________ is a written plan which combines product development, promotion, distribution, and pricing approach, identifies the firm's marketing goals, and explains how they will be achieved within a stated timeframe.

a. Category management
b. Product bundling
c. Disruptive technology
d. Marketing Strategy

10. _________ is something that a firm can do well and that meets the following three conditions:

Competencies are things that companys execute well across several business units or product sectors.

Firms usually have few competencies, but these are usually less liable to change rapidly.

1. It provides consumer benefits
2. It is not easy for competitors to imitate
3. It can be leveraged widely to many products and markets.

A _________ can take various forms, including technical/subject matter know-how, a reliable process and/or close relationships with customers and suppliers (Mascarenhas et al. 1998.)

a. NAIRU
b. Core competency
c. Learning-by-doing
d. Dominant Design

11. _________ is one of the four growth strategies of the Product-Market Growth Matrix defined by Ansoff. _________ occurs when a company enters/penetrates a market with current products. The best way to achieve this is by gaining competitors' customers (part of their market share.)

a. Market penetration
b. 1990 Clean Air Act
c. 33 Strategies of War
d. 28-hour day

12. _________ is subcontracting a process, such as product design or manufacturing, to a third-party company. The decision to outsource is often made in the interest of lowering cost or making better use of time and energy costs, redirecting or conserving energy directed at the competencies of a particular business, or to make more efficient use of land, labor, capital, (information) technology and resources. _________ became part of the business lexicon during the 1980s.

a. Opinion leadership
b. Operant conditioning
c. Outsourcing
d. Unemployment insurance

13. A _________ strategy targets non-buying customers in currently targeted segments. It also targets new customers in new segments. (Winer)

A marketing manager has to think about the following questions before implementing a _________ strategy: Is it profitable? Will it require the introduction of new or modified products? Is the customer and channel well enough researched and understood?

The marketing manager uses these four groups to give more focus to the market segment decision: existing customers, competitor customers, non-buying in current segments, new segments.

a. Context analysis
b. Customer relationship management
c. Product line
d. Market development

14. In business and engineering, new _________ is the term used to describe the complete process of bringing a new product or service to market. There are two parallel paths involved in the NProduct development process: one involves the idea generation, product design, and detail engineering; the other involves market research and marketing analysis. Companies typically see new _________ as the first stage in generating and commercializing new products within the overall strategic process of product life cycle management used to maintain or grow their market share.

a. 28-hour day
b. 1990 Clean Air Act
c. 33 Strategies of War
d. Product development

15. In economics, business, retail, and accounting, a _________ is the value of money that has been used up to produce something, and hence is not available for use anymore. In economics, a _________ is an alternative that is given up as a result of a decision. In business, the _________ may be one of acquisition, in which case the amount of money expended to acquire it is counted as _________.

a. Cost allocation
b. Fixed costs
c. Cost overrun
d. Cost

16. _________ is a concept developed by Michael Porter, used in business strategy. It describes a way to establish the competitive advantage. _________, in basic words, means the lowest cost of operation in the industry.

a. Strategic group
b. Strategic business unit
c. Switching cost
d. Cost leadership

17. _________ has been described as the 'process of social influence in which one person can enlist the aid and support of others in the accomplishment of a common task' . A definition more inclusive of followers comes from Alan Keith of Genentech who said '_________ is ultimately about creating a way for people to contribute to making something extraordinary happen.'

_________ is one of the most salient aspects of the organizational context. However, defining _________ has been challenging.

a. 28-hour day
b. Leadership
c. Situational leadership
d. 1990 Clean Air Act

1. _________ can be regarded as an outcome of mental processes (cognitive process) leading to the selection of a course of action among several alternatives. Every _________ process produces a final choice. The output can be an action or an opinion of choice.

a. 1990 Clean Air Act
b. 33 Strategies of War
c. 28-hour day
d. Decision making

2. _________ is a way of expressing knowledge or belief that an event will occur or has occurred. In mathematics the concept has been given an exact meaning in _________ theory, that is used extensively in such areas of study as mathematics, statistics, finance, gambling, science, and philosophy to draw conclusions about the likelihood of potential events and the underlying mechanics of complex systems.

The word _________ does not have a consistent direct definition.

a. Time series analysis
b. Standard deviation
c. Statistics
d. Probability

3. In decision theory and estimation theory, the _________ of an estimator, $\hat{\theta}$, of an unknown parameter of the distribution, θ, is the expected value of the loss function

$$R(\theta, \hat{\theta}) = \mathbb{E}_\theta L(\theta, \hat{\theta}) = \int L(\theta, \hat{\theta}) \, dP_\theta.$$

where dP_θ is a probability measure parametrized by θ.

- For a scalar parameter θ and a quadratic loss function,

$$L(\theta,\hat{\theta}) = (\theta - \hat{\theta})^2$$

the _________ function becomes the mean squared error of the estimate,

$$R(\theta,\hat{\theta}) = E_\theta(\theta - \hat{\theta})^2$$

- In density estimation, the unknown parameter is probability density itself. The loss function is typically chosen to be a norm in an appropriate function space. For example, for L^2 norm,

$$L(f,\hat{f}) = \|f - \hat{f}\|_2^2$$

the _________ function becomes the mean integrated squared error

$$R(f,\hat{f}) = E\|f - \hat{f}\|^2$$

.

a. Linear model
b. Risk aversion
c. Financial modeling
d. Risk

4. In sociology, anthropology and cultural studies, a _________ is a group of people with a culture (whether distinct or hidden) which differentiates them from the larger culture to which they belong. If a particular _________ is characterized by a systematic opposition to the dominant culture, it may be described as a counterculture.

As early as 1950, David Riesman distinguished between a majority, 'which passively accepted commercially provided styles and meanings, and a '_________' which actively sought a minority style ...

a. 28-hour day
b. 1990 Clean Air Act
c. 33 Strategies of War
d. Subculture

5. In probability theory, a probability distribution is called _________ if its cumulative distribution function is _________. This is equivalent to saying that for random variables X with the distribution in question, Pr[X = a] = 0 for all real numbers a, i.e.: the probability that X attains the value a is zero, for any number a. If the distribution of X is _________ then X is called a _________ random variable.

a. Decision tree pruning
b. Connectionist expert systems
c. Pay Band
d. Continuous

6. _________ is a management process whereby delivery (customer valued) processes are constantly evaluated and improved in the light of their efficiency, effectiveness and flexibility.

Some see it as a meta process for most management systems (Business Process Management, Quality Management, Project Management). Deming saw it as part of the 'system' whereby feedback from the process and customer were evaluated against organisational goals.

a. Sole proprietorship
b. First-mover advantage
c. Critical Success Factor
d. Continuous Improvement Process

7. _________ of the learning curve effect and the closely related experience curve effect express the relationship between equations for experience and efficiency or between efficiency gains and investment in the effort. The experience of 'learning curves' was first observed by the 19th Century German psychologist Hermann Ebbinghaus according to the difficulty of memorizing varying numbers of verbal stimuli, and subsequent learning about the complex processes of learning are discussed in the

.

The rule used for representing the learning curve effect states that the more times a task has been performed, the less time will be required on each subsequent iteration.

a. Spatial Decision Support Systems
b. Distribution
c. Point biserial correlation coefficient
d. Models

8. _________ is a concept based on the fact that rationality of individuals is limited by the information they have, the cognitive limitations of their minds, and the finite amount of time they have to make decisions. This contrasts with the concept of rationality as optimization. Another way to look at _________ is that, because decision-makers lack the ability and resources to arrive at the optimal solution, they instead apply their rationality only after having greatly simplified the choices available.

a. Bounded rationality
b. Complete information
c. Mixed strategy
d. Transferable utility

9. A _________ is an alliance among individuals or groups, during which they cooperate in joint action, each in his own self-interest, joining forces together for a common cause. This alliance may be temporary or a matter of convenience. A _________ thus differs from a more formal covenant.

a. 1990 Clean Air Act
b. 33 Strategies of War
c. Coalition
d. 28-hour day

1. _________ comprises a range of practices used in an organisation to identify, create, represent, distribute and enable adoption of insights and experiences. Such insights and experiences comprise knowledge, either embodied in individuals or embedded in organisational processes or practice.

An established discipline since 1991 , _________ includes courses taught in the fields of business administration, information systems, management, and library and information sciences .

a. 1990 Clean Air Act
b. Knowledge management
c. 33 Strategies of War
d. 28-hour day

2. An _________ is software that attempts to reproduce the performance of one or more human experts, most commonly in a specific problem domain, and is a traditional application and/or subfield of artificial intelligence. A wide variety of methods can be used to simulate the performance of the expert however common to most or all are 1) the creation of a so-called 'knowledgebase' which uses some knowledge representation formalism to capture the Subject Matter Experts (SME) knowledge and 2) a process of gathering that knowledge from the SME and codifying it according to the formalism, which is called knowledge engineering. _________s may or may not have learning components but a third common element is that once the system is developed it is proven by being placed in the same real world problem solving situation as the human SME, typically as an aid to human workers or a supplement to some information system.

a. A4e
b. AAAI
c. A Stake in the Outcome
d. Expert system

3. _________ is the process of estimation in unknown situations. Prediction is a similar, but more general term. Both can refer to estimation of time series, cross-sectional or longitudinal data.

a. 28-hour day
b. 1990 Clean Air Act
c. Forecasting
d. 33 Strategies of War

4. The _________ is a systematic, interactive forecasting method which relies on a panel of independent experts. The carefully selected experts answer questionnaires in two or more rounds. After each round, a facilitator provides an anonymous summary of the experts' forecasts from the previous round as well as the reasons they provided for their judgments.

a. Quality function deployment
b. Learning organization
c. Hoshin Kanri
d. Delphi method

5. _________ is a group creativity technique designed to generate a large number of ideas for the solution of a problem. The method was first popularized in the late 1930s by Alex Faickney Osborn in a book called Applied Imagination. Osborn proposed that groups could double their creative output with _________.
a. Brainstorming
b. Affiliation
c. Abraham Harold Maslow
d. Adam Smith

6. _________ is the process of comparing the cost, cycle time, productivity, or quality of a specific process or method to another that is widely considered to be an industry standard or best practice. Essentially, _________ provides a snapshot of the performance of your business and helps you understand where you are in relation to a particular standard. The result is often a business case for making changes in order to make improvements.
a. Complementors
b. Cost leadership
c. Competitive heterogeneity
d. Benchmarking

7. _________ ('Plan-Do-Check-Act') is an iterative four-step problem-solving process typically used in business process improvement. It is also known as the Deming Cycle, Shewhart cycle, Deming Wheel, or Plan-Do-Study-Act.

_________ was made popular by Dr. W. Edwards Deming, who is considered by many to be the father of modern quality control; however it was always referred to by him as the Shewhart cycle. Later in Deming's career, he modified _________ to Plan, Do, Study, Act (PDSA) so as to better describe his recommendations.

a. Decentralization
b. Management team
c. Management by exception
d. PDCA

8. The _________ is a performance management tool for measuring whether the smaller-scale operational activities of a company are aligned with its larger-scale objectives in terms of vision and strategy.

By focusing not only on financial outcomes but also on the operational, marketing and developmental inputs to these, the _________ helps provide a more comprehensive view of a business, which in turn helps organizations act in their best long-term interests. This tool is also being used to address business response to climate change and greenhouse gas emissions.

a. Middle management
b. Commercial management
c. Balanced scorecard
d. Management development

1. _________ is one of the managerial functions like planning, organizing, staffing and directing. It is an important function because it helps to check the errors and to take the corrective action so that deviation from standards are minimized and stated goals of the organization are achieved in desired manner.According to modern concepts, _________ is a foreseeing action whereas earlier concept of _________ was used only when errors were detected. _________ in management means setting standards, measuring actual performance and taking corrective action.

   a. Control
   b. Decision tree pruning
   c. Schedule of reinforcement
   d. Turnover

2. According to the American Marketing Association, _________ is the marketing of products that are presumed to be environmentally safe. Thus _________ incorporates a broad range of activities, including product modification, changes to the production process, packaging changes, as well as modifying advertising. Yet defining _________ is not a simple task where several meanings intersect and contradict each other; an example of this will be the existence of varying social, environmental and retail definitions attached to this term.

   a. Market share
   b. SWOT analysis
   c. Value chain
   d. Green marketing

3. _________ is an integrated communications-based process through which individuals and communities discover that existing and newly-identified needs and wants may be satisfied by the products and services of others.

_________ is defined by the American _________ Association as the activity, set of institutions, and processes for creating, communicating, delivering, and exchanging offerings that have value for customers, clients, partners, and society at large. The term developed from the original meaning which referred literally to going to market, as in shopping, or going to a market to buy or sell goods or services.

   a. Marketing
   b. Market development
   c. Customer relationship management
   d. Disruptive technology

4. _________ is a term that refers both to:

- a formal discipline used to help appraise, or assess, the case for a project or proposal, which itself is a process known as project appraisal; and
- an informal approach to making decisions of any kind.

Under both definitions the process involves, whether explicitly or implicitly, weighing the total expected costs against the total expected benefits of one or more actions in order to choose the best or most profitable option. The formal process is often referred to as either CBA (_________) or BCost-benefit analysis

A hallmark of CBA is that all benefits and all costs are expressed in money terms, and are adjusted for the time value of money, so that all flows of benefits and flows of project costs over time (which tend to occur at different points in time) are expressed on a common basis in terms of their 'present value.' Closely related, but slightly different, formal techniques include Cost-effectiveness analysis, Economic impact analysis, Fiscal impact analysis and Social Return on Investment(SROI) analysis. The latter builds upon the logic of _________, but differs in that it is explicitly designed to inform the practical decision-making of enterprise managers and investors focused on optimising their social and environmental impacts.

a. Decision engineering
b. Kepner-Tregoe
c. Gittins index
d. Cost-benefit analysis

5. The _________ is a financial ratio that measures whether or not a firm has enough resources to pay its debts over the next 12 months. It compares a firm's current assets to its current liabilities. It is expressed as follows:

$$\text{Current ratio} = \frac{\text{Current Assets}}{\text{Current Liabilities}}$$

For example, if WXY Company's current assets are $50,000,000 and its current liabilities are $40,000,000, then its _________ would be $50,000,000 divided by $40,000,000, which equals 1.25.

a. Financial ratio
b. Return on assets
c. Times interest earned
d. Current ratio

6. _________ is a financial ratio that indicates the percentage of a company's assets are provided via debt. It is the ratio of total debt (the sum of current liabilities and long-term liabilities) and total assets (the sum of current assets, fixed assets, and other assets such as 'goodwill'.)

$$\text{Debt ratio} = \frac{\text{Total Debt}}{\text{Total Assets}}$$

or alternatively:

$$\text{Debt ratio} = \frac{\text{Total Liability}}{\text{Total Assets}}$$

For example, a company with $2 million in total assets and $500,000 in total liabilities would have a _________ of 25%

Like all financial ratios, a company's _________ should be compared with their industry average or other competing firms.

a. 1990 Clean Air Act
b. Demand forecasting
c. 28-hour day
d. Debt ratio

7. In finance, a _________ or accounting ratio is a ratio of two selected numerical values taken from an enterprise's financial statements. There are many standard ratios used to try to evaluate the overall financial condition of a corporation or other organization. _________s may be used by managers within a firm, by current and potential shareholders (owners) of a firm, and by a firm's creditors.

a. Financial ratio
b. Return on sales
c. Rate of return
d. Return on equity

8. The _________ is an equation that equals the cost of goods sold divided by the average inventory. Average inventory equals beginning inventory plus ending inventory divided by 2.

The formula for _________:

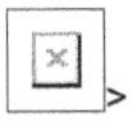>

The formula for average inventory:

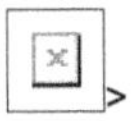>

A low turnover rate may point to overstocking, obsolescence, or deficiencies in the product line or marketing effort.

a. A Stake in the Outcome
b. A4e
c. Asset turnover
d. Inventory turnover

9. _________ is an idea in the field of Organizational studies and management which describes the psychology, attitudes, experiences, beliefs and Values (personal and cultural values) of an organization. It has been defined as 'the specific collection of values and norms that are shared by people and groups in an organization and that control the way they interact with each other and with stakeholders outside the organization.'

This definition continues to explain organizational values also known as 'beliefs and ideas about what kinds of goals members of an organization should pursue and ideas about the appropriate kinds or standards of behavior organizational members should use to achieve these goals. From organizational values develop organizational norms, guidelines or expectations that prescribe appropriate kinds of behavior by employees in particular situations and control the behavior of organizational members towards one another.'

_________ is not the same as corporate culture.

a. Organizational development
b. Organizational culture
c. Organizational effectiveness
d. Union shop

10. _________ refers to an assessment of the viability, stability and profitability of a business, sub-business or project.

It is performed by professionals who prepare reports using ratios that make use of information taken from financial statements and other reports. These reports are usually presented to top management as one of their bases in making business decisions.

a. 28-hour day
b. 33 Strategies of War
c. 1990 Clean Air Act
d. Financial analysis

11. In a human resources context, _________ or labor _________ is the rate at which an employer gains and loses employees. Simple ways to describe it are 'how long employees tend to stay' or 'the rate of traffic through the revolving door.' _________ is measured for individual companies and for their industry as a whole. If an employer is said to have a high _________ relative to its competitors, it means that employees of that company have a shorter average tenure than those of other companies in the same industry.

a. Ten year occupational employment projection
b. Continuous
c. Turnover
d. Career portfolios

12. _________ generally refers to a list of all planned expenses and revenues. It is a plan for saving and spending. A _________ is an important concept in microeconomics, which uses a _________ line to illustrate the trade-offs between two or more goods.

a. 33 Strategies of War
b. 1990 Clean Air Act
c. Budget
d. 28-hour day

13. _________ is a costing model that identifies activities in an organization and assigns the cost of each activity resource to all products and services according to the actual consumption by each: it assigns more indirect costs (overhead) into direct costs.

In this way an organization can establish the true cost of its individual products and services for the purposes of identifying and eliminating those which are unprofitable and lowering the prices of those which are overpriced.

In a business organization, the ABC methodology assigns an organization's resource costs through activities to the products and services provided to its customers.

a. Indirect costs
b. Activity-based costing
c. A4e
d. A Stake in the Outcome

14. _________ is the planning process used to determine whether a firm's long term investments such as new machinery, replacement machinery, new plants, new products, and research development projects are worth pursuing. It is budget for major capital, or investment, expenditures.

Many formal methods are used in _________, including the techniques such as

- Net present value
- Profitability index
- Internal rate of return
- Modified Internal Rate of Return
- Equivalent annuity

These methods use the incremental cash flows from each potential investment, or project. Techniques based on accounting earnings and accounting rules are sometimes used - though economists consider this to be improper - such as the accounting rate of return, and 'return on investment.' Simplified and hybrid methods are used as well, such as payback period and discounted payback period.

a. Restricted stock
b. Gross profit
c. Gross profit margin
d. Capital budgeting

15. In economics, business, retail, and accounting, a _________ is the value of money that has been used up to produce something, and hence is not available for use anymore. In economics, a _________ is an alternative that is given up as a result of a decision. In business, the _________ may be one of acquisition, in which case the amount of money expended to acquire it is counted as _________.
a. Cost
b. Cost allocation
c. Cost overrun
d. Fixed costs

16. The phrase _________, according to the Organization for Economic Co-operation and Development, refers to 'creative work undertaken on a systematic basis in order to increase the stock of knowledge, including knowledge of man, culture and society, and the use of this stock of knowledge to devise new applications [sic]'

New product design and development is more than often a crucial factor in the survival of a company. In an industry that is fast changing, firms must continually revise their design and range of products. This is necessary due to continuous technology change and development as well as other competitors and the changing preference of customers.

a. Research and development
b. 33 Strategies of War
c. 1990 Clean Air Act
d. 28-hour day

17. _________ is the use of control systems (such as numerical control, programmable logic control, and other industrial control systems), in concert with other applications of information technology (such as computer-aided technologies [CAD, CAM, CAx]), to control industrial machinery and processes, reducing the need for human intervention. In the scope of industrialization, _________ is a step beyond mechanization. Whereas mechanization provided human operators with machinery to assist them with the physical requirements of work, _________ greatly reduces the need for human sensory and mental requirements as well.
a. A Stake in the Outcome
b. Automation
c. AAAI
d. A4e

18. An _________ is a meeting that official bodies, and associations involving the public, are often required by law to hold.

An _________ is generally held every year to inform their members of previous and future activities. It is an opportunity for the shareholders and partners to receive copies of the company's accounts as well as reviewing fiscal information for the past year and asking any questions regarding the decisions the business will take in the future.

a. A Stake in the Outcome
b. A4e
c. AAAI
d. Annual general meeting

19. An _________ is a comprehensive report on a company's activities throughout the preceding year. _________s are intended to give shareholders and other interested persons information about the company's activities and financial performance. Most jurisdictions require companies to prepare and disclose _________s, and many require the _________ to be filed at the company's registry.
a. Annual report
b. AAAI
c. A4e
d. A Stake in the Outcome

20. A _________ is a body of elected or appointed members who jointly oversee the activities of a company or organization. The body sometimes has a different name, such as board of trustees, board of governors, board of managers, or executive board. It is often simply referred to as 'the board.'

A board's activities are determined by the powers, duties, and responsibilities delegated to it or conferred on it by an authority outside itself.

a. Foreign Corrupt Practices Act
b. Clean Water Act
c. Competition law
d. Board of directors

21. _________ can refer to a law of local or limited application, passed under the authority of a higher law specifying what things may be regulated by the _________, or it can refer to the internal rules of a company or organisation.

Corporate and organizational _________s regulate only the organisation to which they apply and are generally concerned with the operation of the organisation, setting out the form, manner or procedure in which a company or organisation should be run. Corporate _________s are drafted by a corporation's founders or directors under the authority of its Charter or Articles of Incorporation.

a. Genuine Occupational Qualification
b. Fiduciary
c. Racketeer Influenced and Corrupt Organizations Act
d. Bylaw

22. _________ is the set of processes, customs, policies, laws, and institutions affecting the way a corporation (or company) is directed, administered or controlled. _________ also includes the relationships among the many stakeholders involved and the goals for which the corporation is governed. The principal stakeholders are the shareholders/members, management, and the board of directors.

a. Flextime
b. Corporate governance
c. No-FEAR Act
d. Guarantee

23. A _________ is a statement required of a United States firm when soliciting shareholder votes. The firm needs to file a _________ with the U.S. Securities and Exchange Commission. This statement is useful in assessing how management is paid and potential conflict-of-interest issues with auditors.

a. 28-hour day
b. 1990 Clean Air Act
c. 33 Strategies of War
d. Proxy statement

24. The _________ of 2002 (Pub.L. 107-204, 116 Stat. 745, enacted July 30, 2002), also known as the Public Company Accounting Reform and Investor Protection Act of 2002 and commonly called Sarbanes-Oxley, Sarbox or SOX, is a United States federal law enacted on July 30, 2002, as a reaction to a number of major corporate and accounting scandals including those affecting Enron, Tyco International, Adelphia, Peregrine Systems and WorldCom.
a. Sarbanes-Oxley Act of 2002
b. Fair Labor Standards Act
c. Letter of credit
d. Sarbanes-Oxley Act

25. _________ is the self-government of a nation, country or some portion thereof, generally exercising sovereignty.

The term _________ is used in contrast to subjugation, which refers to a region as a 'territory' --subject to the political and military control of an external government. The word is sometimes used in a weaker sense to contrast with hegemony, the indirect control of one nation by another, more powerful nation.

a. A4e
b. AAAI
c. A Stake in the Outcome
d. Independence

26. In accounting and auditing, _________ is defined as a process effected by an organization's structure, work and authority flows, people and management information systems, designed to help the organization accomplish specific goals or objectives. It is a means by which an organization's resources are directed, monitored, and measured. It plays an important role in preventing and detecting fraud and protecting the organization's resources, both physical (e.g., machinery and property) and intangible (e.g., reputation or intellectual property such as trademarks.)
a. Audit committee
b. Internal auditing
c. A Stake in the Outcome
d. Internal control

27. A _________ is a person who alleges misconduct. More complex definitions may be used, but the issue is that the _________ usually faces reprisal. The misconduct may be classified in many ways; for example, a violation of a law, rule, regulation and/or a direct threat to public interest, such as fraud, health/safety violations, and corruption.

a. 28-hour day
b. 1990 Clean Air Act
c. 33 Strategies of War
d. Whistleblower

28. A _________ is a research instrument consisting of a series of questions and other prompts for the purpose of gathering information from respondents. Although they are often designed for statistical analysis of the responses, this is not always the case. The _________ was invented by Sir Francis Galton.

a. Questionnaire construction
b. Structured interview
c. Mystery shoppers
d. Questionnaire

1. An _________, or organogram(me)) is a diagram that shows the structure of an organization and the relationships and relative ranks of its parts and positions/jobs. The term is also used for similar diagrams, for example ones showing the different elements of a field of knowledge or a group of languages. The French Encyclopédie had one of the first _________s of knowledge in general.

a. A4e
b. A Stake in the Outcome
c. AAAI
d. Organizational chart

2. _________ is a term originating in military organization theory, but now used more commonly in business management, particularly human resource management. _________ refers to the number of subordinates a supervisor has.

In the hierarchical business organization of the past it was not uncommon to see average spans of 1 to 10 or even less. That is, one manager supervised ten employees on average.

a. Mentoring
b. CIFMS
c. Senior management
d. Span of control

3. _________ is one of the managerial functions like planning, organizing, staffing and directing. It is an important function because it helps to check the errors and to take the corrective action so that deviation from standards are minimized and stated goals of the organization are achieved in desired manner.According to modern concepts, _________ is a foreseeing action whereas earlier concept of _________ was used only when errors were detected. _________ in management means setting standards, measuring actual performance and taking corrective action.

a. Decision tree pruning
b. Schedule of reinforcement
c. Turnover
d. Control

4. _________ is a concept in ethics with several meanings. It is often used synonymously with such concepts as responsibility, answerability, enforcement, blameworthiness, liability and other terms associated with the expectation of account-giving. As an aspect of governance, it has been central to discussions related to problems in both the public and private (corporation) worlds.

a. A Stake in the Outcome
b. Usury
c. Accountability
d. A4e

5. _________ is the process by which the activities of an organisation, particularly those regarding decision-making, become concentrated within a particular location and/or group.

a. Chief operating officer
b. Corner office
c. Product innovation
d. Centralization

6. _________ is the process of dispersing decision-making governance closer to the people or citizen. It includes the dispersal of administration or governance in sectors or areas like engineering, management science, political science, political economy, sociology and economics. _________ is also possible in the dispersal of population and employment.

a. Frenemy
b. Business plan
c. Decentralization
d. Formula for Change

7. _________ can be defined as the idea generation, concept development, testing and manufacturing or implementation of a physical object or service. _________ers conceptualize and evaluate ideas, making them tangible through products in a more systematic approach. The role of a _________er encompasses many characteristics of the marketing manager, product manager, industrial designer and design engineer.

a. Abraham Harold Maslow
b. Adam Smith
c. Affiliation
d. Product design

8. _________ is a dynamic of being mutually and physically responsible to and sharing a common set of principles with others. This concept differs distinctly from 'dependence' in that an interdependent relationship implies that all participants are emotionally, economically, ecologically and or morally 'interdependent.' Some people advocate freedom or independence as a sort of ultimate good; others do the same with devotion to one's family, community, or society. _________ recognizes the truth in each position and weaves them together.

a. AAAI
b. A4e
c. Interdependence
d. A Stake in the Outcome

9. A _________ is a research instrument consisting of a series of questions and other prompts for the purpose of gathering information from respondents. Although they are often designed for statistical analysis of the responses, this is not always the case. The _________ was invented by Sir Francis Galton.

a. Questionnaire
b. Mystery shoppers
c. Structured interview
d. Questionnaire construction

1. _________ is a business management strategy aimed at embedding awareness of quality in all organizational processes. _________ has been widely used in manufacturing, education, hospitals, call centers, government, and service industries, as well as NASA space and science programs.

As defined by the International Organization for Standardization (ISO):

> '_________ is a management approach for an organization, centered on quality, based on the participation of all its members and aiming at long-term success through customer satisfaction, and benefits to all members of the organization and to society.' ISO 8402:1994

One major aim is to reduce variation from every process so that greater consistency of effort is obtained. (Royse, D., Thyer, B., Padgett D., ' Logan T., 2006)

a. 28-hour day
b. 1990 Clean Air Act
c. Total quality management
d. Quality management

2. _________ can be considered to have three main components: quality control, quality assurance and quality improvement. _________ is focused not only on product quality, but also the means to achieve it. _________ therefore uses quality assurance and control of processes as well as products to achieve more consistent quality.

a. 1990 Clean Air Act
b. 28-hour day
c. Total quality management
d. Quality management

3. _________ is a term coined by Deborah E. Meyerson used to describe corporate professionals who work toward positive change in both their work environment and the way their companies conduct business -- often taking 'radical' action that is just short of getting them fired.

In her book, _________: How Everyday Leaders Inspire Change at Work (Harvard Business School Press), Meyerson describes employees who believe and work toward creating adaptive, family-friendly, and socially responsible workplaces.

_________ are quiet leaders that act as catalysts for new ideas, alternative perspectives, and organizational learning and change -- and balance company conformity with individual rebellion.

a. 1990 Clean Air Act
b. 28-hour day
c. Tempered radicals
d. 33 Strategies of War

4. In the field of Organizational Development there are many activities and disciplines. One of those is the area of _________ and the use of structured organizational diagnostic tools.

The effective diagnosis of organizational culture, and structural and operational strengths and weaknesses are fundamental to any successful organizational development intervention.

a. A Stake in the Outcome
b. Organizational diagnosis
c. AAAI
d. A4e

5. _________ is the corporate management term for the act of reorganizing the legal, ownership, operational, or other structures of a company for the purpose of making it more profitable, or better organized for its present needs. Alternate reasons for _________ include a change of ownership or ownership structure, demerger repositioning debt _________ and financial _________.

a. Market value
b. Restructuring
c. Market value added
d. Net worth

6. In mathematical logic, _________ is a valid argument and rule of inference which makes the inference that, if the conjunction A and B is true, then A is true, and B is true.

In formal language:

$$A \wedge B \vdash A$$

or

$$A \wedge B \vdash B$$

The argument has one premise, namely a conjunction, and one often uses _________ in longer arguments to derive one of the conjuncts.

An example in English:

It's raining and it's pouring.

a. Simplification
b. Fuzzy logic
c. Validity
d. 1990 Clean Air Act

7. A _________ is a form of qualitative research in which a group of people are asked about their attitude towards a product, service, concept, advertisement, idea, or packaging. Questions are asked in an interactive group setting where participants are free to talk with other group members.

The first _________s were created at the Bureau of Applied Social Research by associate director, sociologist Robert K. Merton.

a. Focus group
b. Marketing research
c. Market analysis
d. 1990 Clean Air Act

8. _________ is an attempt to motivate employees by giving them the opportunity to use the range of their abilities. It is an idea that was developed by the American psychologist Frederick Herzberg in the 1950s. It can be contrasted to job enlargement which simply increases the number of tasks without changing the challenge.
a. C-A-K-E
b. Cash cow
c. Catfish effect
d. Job enrichment

9. _________. The objective of OD is to improve the organization's capacity to handle its internal and external functioning and relationships. This would include such things as improved interpersonal and group processes, more effective communication, enhanced ability to cope with organizational problems of all kinds, more effective decision processes, more appropriate leadership style, improved skill in dealing with destructive conflict, and higher levels of trust and cooperation among organizational members.

a. Industrial relations
b. Organizational structure
c. Organizational development
d. Improved Organizational Performance

10. _________ describes the situation when output from (or information about the result of) an event or phenomenon in the past will influence the same event/phenomenon in the present or future. When an event is part of a chain of cause-and-effect that forms a circuit or loop, then the event is said to 'feed back' into itself.

_________ is also a synonym for:

- _________ signal; the information about the initial event that is the basis for subsequent modification of the event.
- _________ loop; the causal path that leads from the initial generation of the _________ signal to the subsequent modification of the event.

_________ is a mechanism, process or signal that is looped back to control a system within itself. Such a loop is called a _________ loop.

a. Positive feedback
b. Feedback loop
c. 1990 Clean Air Act
d. Feedback

11. _________ is a company-wide computer software system used to manage and coordinate all the resources, information, and functions of a business from shared data stores.

An _________ system has a service-oriented architecture with modular hardware and software units and 'services' that communicate on a local area network. The modular design allows a business to add or reconfigure modules (perhaps from different vendors) while preserving data integrity in one shared database that may be centralized or distributed.

a. Enterprise resource planning
b. A4e
c. A Stake in the Outcome
d. AAAI

12. A _________ is the term given to a company that facilitates the learning of its members and continuously transforms itself. _________s develop as a result of the pressures facing modern organizations and enables them to remain competitive in the business environment. A _________ has five main features; systems thinking, personal mastery, mental models, shared vision and team learning.

a. Quality function deployment
b. Hoshin Kanri
c. 1990 Clean Air Act
d. Learning organization

13. _________ has been described as the 'process of social influence in which one person can enlist the aid and support of others in the accomplishment of a common task' . A definition more inclusive of followers comes from Alan Keith of Genentech who said '_________ is ultimately about creating a way for people to contribute to making something extraordinary happen.'

_________ is one of the most salient aspects of the organizational context. However, defining _________ has been challenging.

a. Leadership
b. Situational leadership
c. 28-hour day
d. 1990 Clean Air Act

14. _________ refers to increasing the spiritual, political, social or economic strength of individuals and communities. It often involves the empowered developing confidence in their own capacities.

The term Human _________ covers a vast landscape of meanings, interpretations, definitions and disciplines ranging from psychology and philosophy to the highly commercialized Self-Help industry and Motivational sciences.

a. Empowerment
b. AAAI
c. A Stake in the Outcome
d. A4e

1. _________ is an increasingly broadening term with which an organization, or other human system describes the combination of traditionally administrative personnel functions with acquisition and application of skills, knowledge and experience, Employee Relations and resource planning at various levels. The field draws upon concepts developed in Industrial/Organizational Psychology and System Theory. _________ has at least two related interpretations depending on context. The original usage derives from political economy and economics, where it was traditionally called labor, one of four factors of production although this perspective is changing as a function of new and ongoing research into more strategic approaches at national levels. This first usage is used more in terms of '_________ development', and can go beyond just organizations to the level of nations . The more traditional usage within corporations and businesses refers to the individuals within a firm or agency, and to the portion of the organization that deals with hiring, firing, training, and other personnel issues, typically referred to as `_________ management'.

a. Human resources
b. Progressive discipline
c. Bradford Factor
d. Human resource management

2. _________ is, in very basic words, a position a firm occupies against its competitors.

According to Michael Porter, the three methods for creating a sustainable _________ are through:

1. Cost leadership

2. Differentiation

3. Focus (economics)

a. 28-hour day
b. 1990 Clean Air Act
c. Theory Z
d. Competitive advantage

3. _________ is a contract between two parties, one being the employer and the other being the employee. An employee may be defined as: 'A person in the service of another under any contract of hire, express or implied, oral or written, where the employer has the power or right to control and direct the employee in the material details of how the work is to be performed.' Black's Law Dictionary page 471 (5th ed. 1979.)

a. Exit interview
b. Employment rate
c. Employment counsellor
d. Employment

4. The term _________ was created by President Lyndon B. Johnson when he signed Executive Order 11246 on September 24, 1965, created to prohibit federal contractors from discriminating against employees on the basis of race, sex, creed, religion, color, or national origin. In more recent times, most employers have also added sexual orientation to the list of non-discrimination.

The Executive Order also required contractors to implement affirmative action plans to increase the participation of minorities and women in the workplace.

a. AAAI
b. A Stake in the Outcome
c. A4e
d. Equal Employment Opportunity

5. The _________ of 1967, Pub. L. No. 90-202, 81 Stat. 602 (Dec. 15, 1967), codified as Chapter 14 of Title 29 of the United States Code, 29 U.S.C. Â§ 621 through 29 U.S.C. Â§ 634 (ADEA), prohibits employment discrimination against persons 40 years of age or older in the United States). The law also sets standards for pensions and benefits provided by employers and requires that information about the needs of older workers be provided to the general public.

a. Age Discrimination in Employment Act
b. Undue hardship
c. Extra time
d. Unemployment and Farm Relief Act

6. The _________ of 1990 (ADA) is the short title of United States (Pub.L. 101-336, 104 Stat. 327, enacted July 26, 1990), codified at 42 U.S.C. Â§ 12101 et seq. It was signed into law on July 26, 1990, by President George H. W. Bush, and later amended with changes effective January 1, 2009. The ADA is a wide-ranging civil rights law that prohibits, under certain circumstances, discrimination based on disability. It affords similar protections against discrimination to Americans with disabilities as the Civil Rights Act of 1964,

a. Equal Pay Act of 1963
b. Australian labour law
c. Employment discrimination
d. Americans with Disabilities Act

7. The _________ 1970 is an Act of the United Kingdom Parliament which prohibits any less favourable treatment between men and women in terms of pay and conditions of employment. It came into force on 29 December 1975. The term pay is interpreted in a broad sense to include, on top of wages, things like holidays, pension rights, company perks and some kinds of bonuses.

a. Australian labour law
b. Equal Pay Act
c. Architectural Barriers Act of 1968
d. Oncale v. Sundowner Offshore Services

8. The _________ of 1938 (_________, ch. 676, 52 Stat. 1060, June 25, 1938, 29 U.S.C. ch.8), also called the Wages and Hours Bill, is United States federal law that applies to employees engaged in interstate commerce or employed by an enterprise engaged in commerce or in the production of goods for commerce, unless the employer can claim an exemption from coverage. The _________ established a national minimum wage, guaranteed time and a half for overtime in certain jobs, and prohibited most employment of minors in 'oppressive child labor,' a term defined in the statute.
a. Family and Medical Leave Act of 1993
b. Board of directors
c. Fair Labor Standards Act
d. Joint venture

9. The _________ is a United States labor law allowing an employee to take unpaid leave due to a serious health condition that makes the employee unable to perform his job or to care for a sick family member or to care for a new son or daughter (including by birth, adoption or foster care.) The bill was among the first signed into law by President Bill Clinton in his first term.
a. Sarbanes-Oxley Act of 2002
b. Contributory negligence
c. Family and Medical Leave Act of 1993
d. Harvester Judgment

10. _________ are conventions, treaties and recommendations designed to eliminate unjust and inhumane labour practices. The primary inernational agency charged with developing such standards is the International Labour Organization (ILO.) Established in 1919, the ILO advocates international standards as essential for the eradication of labour conditions involving 'injustice, hardship and privation'.
a. Airbus SAS
b. International labour standards
c. Airbus Industrie
d. Anaconda Copper

11. _________ is a cross-disciplinary area concerned with protecting the safety, health and welfare of people engaged in work or employment. The goal of all _________ programs is to foster a work free safe environment. As a secondary effect, it may also protect co-workers, family members, employers, customers, suppliers, nearby communities, and other members of the public who are impacted by the workplace environment.

a. A4e
b. AAAI
c. A Stake in the Outcome
d. Occupational Safety and Health

12. The _________ is the primary federal law which governs occupational health and safety in the private sector and federal government in the United States. It was enacted by Congress in 1970 and was signed by President Richard Nixon on December 29, 1970. Its main goal is to ensure that employers provide employees with an environment free from recognized hazards, such as exposure to toxic chemicals, excessive noise levels, mechanical dangers, heat or cold stress, or unsanitary conditions.
a. United States Department of Justice
b. Unemployment and Farm Relief Act
c. Unemployment Action Center
d. Occupational Safety and Health Act

13. _________ occurs when expectant women are fired, not hired, or otherwise discriminated against due to their pregnancy or intention to become pregnant. Common forms of _________ include not being hired due to visible pregnancy or likelihood of becoming pregnant, being fired after informing an employer of one's pregnancy, being fired after maternity leave, and receiving a pay dock due to pregnancy. In the United States, since 1978, employers are legally bound to provide what insurance, leave pay, and additional support that would be bestowed upon any employee with medical leave or disability.
a. Pregnancy Discrimination
b. 1990 Clean Air Act
c. 33 Strategies of War
d. 28-hour day

14. _________ is the process of learning a new skill or trade, often in response to a change in the economic environment. Generally it reflects changes in profession choice rather than an 'upward' movement in the same field.

There is some controversy surrounding the use of _________ to offset economic changes caused by free trade and automation.

a. Krauthammer
b. Suspension training
c. Compliance Training
d. Retraining

15. The _________ is a United States labor law which protects employees, their families, and communities by requiring most employers with 100 or more employees to provide sixty- (60) calendar-day advance notification of plant closings and mass layoffs of employees. It was enacted in 1989.

Employees entitled to notice under the _________ include managers and supervisors, hourly wage, and salaried workers.

a. Robinson-Patman Act
b. Non-disclosure agreement
c. Leave of absence
d. Worker Adjustment and Retraining Notification Act

16. _________ is the temporary suspension or permanent termination of employment of an employee or (more commonly) a group of employees for business reasons, such as the decision that certain positions are no longer necessary or a business slow-down or interruption in work. Originally the term '_________' referred exclusively to a temporary interruption in work, as when factory work cyclically falls off. However, in recent times the term can also refer to the permanent elimination of a position.

a. Termination of employment
b. Retirement
c. Wrongful dismissal
d. Layoff

17. _________ is an internal recruitment method employed by organisations to identify potential candidates from their existing employees social networks. An _________ scheme encourages a company's existing employees to select and recruit the suitable candidates from their social networks. As a reward, the employer typically pays the referring employee a referral bonus.

a. Employment agency
b. Internet recruiting
c. Executive search
d. Employee referral

18. _________ refers to the process of screening, and selecting qualified people for a job at an organization or firm mid- and large-size organizations and companies often retain professional recruiters or outsource some of the process to _________ agencies. External _________ is the process of attracting and selecting employees from outside the organization.

The _________ industry has four main types of agencies: employment agencies, _________ websites and job search engines, 'headhunters' for executive and professional _________, and in-house _________.

a. Labour hire
b. Recruitment
c. Referral recruitment
d. Recruitment Process Outsourcing

19. Performance Testing covers a broad range of engineering or functional evaluations where a material, product, system emphasis is on the final measurable performance characteristics.

Performance testing can refer to the assessment of the performance of a human examinee. For example, a behind-the-wheel driving test is a _________ of whether a person is able to perform the functions of a competent driver of an automobile.

a. Reverse engineering
b. 1990 Clean Air Act
c. 28-hour day
d. Performance test

20. _________ is a term defined by the Oxford English Dictionary as an individual's 'course or progress through life '. It is usually considered to pertain to remunerative work (and sometimes also formal education.)

The etymology of the term is somewhat ironic in that it comes from the Latin word carrera, which means race .

a. Nursing shortage
b. Spatial mismatch
c. Career planning
d. Career

21. In organizational development (or OD), the study of _________ looks at:

- how individuals manage their careers within and between organizations
- and how organizations structure the career progress of their members, it can also be tied into succession planning within some organizations.

In personal development, _________ is:

- '... the total constellation of psychological, sociological, educational, physical, economic, and chance factors that combine to influence the nature and significance of work in the total lifespan of any given individual.'
- '... the lifelong psychological and behavioral processes as well as contextual influences shaping one's career over the life span. As such, _________ involves the person's creation of a career pattern, decision-making style, integration of life roles, values expression, and life-role self concepts.'

Figures in _________

- Jeff A. Brown
- Jesse B. Davis
- Caela Farren
- John L. Holland
- Kris Magnusson
- Frank Parsons
- Vance Peavy
- Edgar Schein
- Rino Schreuder
- Mark L. Savickas
- Donald Super

.

a. Sole proprietorship
b. Business process reengineering
c. Career development
d. Horizontal integration

22. There are two types of _________ relationships: formal and informal. Informal relationships develop on their own between partners. Formal _________, on the other hand, refers to assigned relationships, often associated with organizational _________ programs designed to promote employee development or to assist at-risk children and youth.

a. Human resource management system
b. Fix it twice
c. Real Property Administrator
d. Mentoring

23. _________ is a method by which the job performance of an employee is evaluated _________ is a part of career development.

_________s are regular reviews of employee performance within organizations

Generally, the aims of a _________ are to:

- Give feedback on performance to employees.
- Identify employee training needs.
- Document criteria used to allocate organizational rewards.
- Form a basis for personnel decisions: salary increases, promotions, disciplinary actions, etc.
- Provide the opportunity for organizational diagnosis and development.
- Facilitate communication between employee and administraton
- Validate selection techniques and human resource policies to meet federal Equal Employment Opportunity requirements.

A common approach to assessing performance is to use a numerical or scalar rating system whereby managers are asked to score an individual against a number of objectives/attributes. In some companies, employees receive assessments from their manager, peers, subordinates and customers while also performing a self assessment.

a. Human resource management
b. Personnel management
c. Progressive discipline
d. Performance appraisal

24. The _________ system was developed by AMD in the mid-1990s as a method of comparing their x86 processors to those of rival Intel.

The first use of the _________ system was in 1996, when AMD used it to assert that their AMD 5x86 processor was as fast as a Pentium running at 75 MHz. The designation 'P75' was added to the chip to denote this.

a. 33 Strategies of War
b. Performance rating
c. 1990 Clean Air Act
d. 28-hour day

25. In the fields of science, engineering, industry and statistics, _________ is the degree of closeness of a measured or calculated quantity to its actual (true) value. _________ is closely related to precision, also called reproducibility or repeatability, the degree to which further measurements or calculations show the same or similar results. _________ indicates proximity to the true value, precision to the repeatability or reproducibility of the measurement

The results of calculations or a measurement can be accurate but not precise, precise but not accurate, neither, or both.

a. AAAI
b. A4e
c. A Stake in the Outcome
d. Accuracy

26. _________ describes the situation when output from (or information about the result of) an event or phenomenon in the past will influence the same event/phenomenon in the present or future. When an event is part of a chain of cause-and-effect that forms a circuit or loop, then the event is said to 'feed back' into itself.

_________ is also a synonym for:

- _________ signal; the information about the initial event that is the basis for subsequent modification of the event.
- _________ loop; the causal path that leads from the initial generation of the _________ signal to the subsequent modification of the event.

_________ is a mechanism, process or signal that is looped back to control a system within itself. Such a loop is called a _________ loop.

a. Positive feedback
b. Feedback loop
c. 1990 Clean Air Act
d. Feedback

27. A _________ is a set of categories designed to elicit information about a quantitative or a qualitative attribute. In the social sciences, common examples are the Likert scale and 1-10 _________s in which a person selects the number which is considered to reflect the perceived quality of a product.

A _________ is an instrument that requires the rater to assign the rated object that have numerals assigned to them.

a. Rating scale
b. Polytomous Rasch model
c. Spearman-Brown prediction formula
d. Thurstone scale

28. _________ and benefits in kind are various non-wage compensations provided to employees in addition to their normal wages or salaries. Where an employee exchanges (cash) wages for some other form of benefit, this is generally referred to as a 'salary sacrifice' arrangement. In most countries, most kinds of _________ are taxable to at least some degree.

a. A4e

b. A Stake in the Outcome

c. Interactive Accommodation Process

d. Employee benefits

29. In economics and sociology, an _________ is any factor (financial or non-financial) that enables or motivates a particular course of action, or counts as a reason for preferring one choice to the alternatives. It is an expectation that encourages people to behave in a certain way. Since human beings are purposeful creatures, the study of _________ structures is central to the study of all economic activity (both in terms of individual decision-making and in terms of co-operation and competition within a larger institutional structure.)

a. AAAI

b. A Stake in the Outcome

c. Incentive

d. A4e

30. A _________ is a research instrument consisting of a series of questions and other prompts for the purpose of gathering information from respondents. Although they are often designed for statistical analysis of the responses, this is not always the case. The _________ was invented by Sir Francis Galton.

a. Mystery shoppers

b. Questionnaire construction

c. Structured interview

d. Questionnaire

1. In organizational development (OD), _________ is the application of Socio-Technical Systems principles and techniques to the humanization of work.

The aims of _________ to improved job satisfaction, to improved through-put, to improved quality and to reduced employee problems, e.g., grievances, absenteeism.

Under scientific management people would be directed by reason and the problems of industrial unrest would be appropriately (i.e., scientifically) addressed.

a. Path-goal theory
b. Management process
c. Graduate recruitment
d. Work design

2. A _________ is the term given to a company that facilitates the learning of its members and continuously transforms itself. _________s develop as a result of the pressures facing modern organizations and enables them to remain competitive in the business environment. A _________ has five main features; systems thinking, personal mastery, mental models, shared vision and team learning.

a. Quality function deployment
b. Hoshin Kanri
c. Learning organization
d. 1990 Clean Air Act

3. _________ has become one of the most popular theories in organizational psychology.

Goal setting has been a formula used for acheivement since the early 1800s. The form and pattern has cahanged drastically over the years and there is still much debate as to what is the most efective pattern to follow.

a. Human relations
b. Goal-setting theory
c. Corporate Culture
d. Job satisfaction

4. _________ is a process of agreeing upon objectives within an organization so that management and employees agree to the objectives and understand what they are in the organization.

The term '_________' was first popularized by Peter Drucker in his 1954 book 'The Practice of Management'.

The essence of _________ is participative goal setting, choosing course of actions and decision making.

a. Business economics
b. Job enrichment
c. Management by objectives
d. Clean sheet review

5. _________ is the use of empirically demonstrated behavior change techniques to improve behavior, such as altering an individual's behaviors and reactions to stimuli through positive and negative reinforcement of adaptive behavior and/or the reduction of maladaptive behavior through punishment and/or therapy.

The first use of the term _________ appears to have been by Edward Thorndike in 1911

a. 1990 Clean Air Act
b. 28-hour day
c. 33 Strategies of War
d. Behavior modification

6. In economics and sociology, an _________ is any factor (financial or non-financial) that enables or motivates a particular course of action, or counts as a reason for preferring one choice to the alternatives. It is an expectation that encourages people to behave in a certain way. Since human beings are purposeful creatures, the study of _________ structures is central to the study of all economic activity (both in terms of individual decision-making and in terms of co-operation and competition within a larger institutional structure.)
a. AAAI
b. A4e
c. A Stake in the Outcome
d. Incentive

7. In operant conditioning, _________ occurs when an event following a response causes an increase in the probability of that response occurring in the future. Response strength can be assessed by measures such as the frequency with which the response is made (for example, a pigeon may peck a key more times in the session), or the speed with which it is made (for example, a rat may run a maze faster.) The environment change contingent upon the response is called a reinforcer.
a. Reinforcement
b. Historiometry
c. Meetings, Incentives, Conferences, and Exhibitions
d. Diminishing Manufacturing Sources and Material Shortages

8. _________ is about the mental processes regarding choice, or choosing. It explains the processes that an individual undergoes to make choices. In organizational behavior study, _________ is a motivation theory first proposed by Victor Vroom of the Yale School of Management.

a. AAAI
b. Expectancy theory
c. A Stake in the Outcome
d. A4e

9. _________ describes the situation when output from (or information about the result of) an event or phenomenon in the past will influence the same event/phenomenon in the present or future. When an event is part of a chain of cause-and-effect that forms a circuit or loop, then the event is said to 'feed back' into itself.

_________ is also a synonym for:

- _________ signal; the information about the initial event that is the basis for subsequent modification of the event.
- _________ loop; the causal path that leads from the initial generation of the _________ signal to the subsequent modification of the event.

_________ is a mechanism, process or signal that is looped back to control a system within itself. Such a loop is called a _________ loop.

a. 1990 Clean Air Act
b. Feedback loop
c. Positive feedback
d. Feedback

10. _________ are job factors that can cause dissatisfaction if missing but do not necessarily motivate employees if increased.

_________ have mostly to do with the job environment. These factors are important or notable only when they are lacking.

a. Work-at-home scheme
b. Hygiene factors
c. Split shift
d. Work system

11. _________ was developed by Frederick Herzberg, a psychologist who found that job satisfaction and job dissatisfaction acted independently of each other. _________ states that there are certain factors in the workplace that cause job satisfaction, while a separate set of factors cause dissatisfaction.

a. Need for power
b. Need for Achievement
c. 1990 Clean Air Act
d. Two-factor theory

12. _________ attempts to explain relational satisfaction in terms of perceptions of fair/unfair distributions of resources within interpersonal relationships. _________ is considered as one of the justice theories, It was first developed in 1962 by John Stacey Adams, a workplace and behavioral psychologist, who asserted that employees seek to maintain equity between the inputs that they bring to a job and the outcomes that they receive from it against the perceived inputs and outcomes of others (Adams, 1965.) The belief is that people value fair treatment which causes them to be motivated to keep the fairness maintained within the relationships of their co-workers and the organization.
a. AAAI
b. A Stake in the Outcome
c. A4e
d. Equity theory

13. Maslow's _________ is a theory in psychology, proposed by Abraham Maslow in his 1943 paper A Theory of Human Motivation, which he subsequently extended to include his observations of humans' innate curiosity.

Maslow's _________ is predetermined in order of importance. It is often depicted as a pyramid consisting of five levels: the lowest level is associated with physiological needs, while the uppermost level is associated with self-actualization needs, particularly those related to identity and purpose. Deficiency needs must be met first. Once these are met, seeking to satisfy growth needs drives personal growth. The higher needs in this hierarchy only come into focus when the lower needs in the pyramid are met.

a. 33 Strategies of War
b. 1990 Clean Air Act
c. Hierarchy of needs
d. 28-hour day

14. In law, _________ is the term to describe a partnership between two or more parties.

In England a number of statutes on the subject have been passed, the chief being the Bastardy Act of 1845, and the Bastardy Laws Amendment Acts of 1872 and 1873. The mother of a bastard may summon the putative father to petty sessions within twelve months of the birth (or at any later time if he is proved to have contributed to the child's support within twelve months after the birth), and the justices, as after hearing evidence on both sides, may, if the mother's evidence be corroborated in some material particular, adjudge the man to be the putative father of the child, and order him to pay a sum not exceeding five shillings a week for its maintenance, together with a sum for expenses incidental to the birth, or the funeral expenses, if it has died before the date of order, and the costs of the proceedings.

a. Affiliation
b. Abraham Harold Maslow
c. Adam Smith
d. Affiliation

15. _________ is a term that has been used in various psychology theories, often in slightly different ways (e.g., Goldstein, Maslow, Rogers.) The term was originally introduced by the organismic theorist Kurt Goldstein for the motive to realise all of one's potentialities. In his view, it is the master motive--indeed, the only real motive a person has, all others being merely manifestations of it.

a. 1990 Clean Air Act
b. Self-actualization
c. 33 Strategies of War
d. 28-hour day

1. _________ has been described as the 'process of social influence in which one person can enlist the aid and support of others in the accomplishment of a common task' . A definition more inclusive of followers comes from Alan Keith of Genentech who said '_________ is ultimately about creating a way for people to contribute to making something extraordinary happen.'

_________ is one of the most salient aspects of the organizational context. However, defining _________ has been challenging.

a. Situational leadership
b. 1990 Clean Air Act
c. Leadership
d. 28-hour day

2. _________ , often measured as an _________ Quotient (EQ), is a term that describes the ability, capacity, skill or (in the case of the trait _________ model) a self-perceived ability, to identify, assess, and manage the emotions of one's self, of others, and of groups. Different models have been proposed for the definition of _________ and disagreement exists as to how the term should be used. Despite these disagreements, which are often highly technical, the ability _________ and trait _________ models (but not the mixed models) are enjoying considerable support in the literature and have successful applications in many different domains.

a. A4e
b. A Stake in the Outcome
c. AAAI
d. Emotional intelligence

3. Social consciousness is consciousness shared within a society. It can also be defined as _________; to be aware of the problems that different societies and communities face on a day-to-day basis; to be conscious of the difficulties and hardships of society.

There is debate as to exactly what the term means.

a. Role conflict
b. Soft skill
c. Self-disclosure
d. Social awareness

4. In behaviorial science, system theory and dynamic systems modeling, a _________ reproduces the required behavior of the original analyzed system, such as there is a one-to-one correspondence between the behavior of the original system and the simulated system. That namely implies that the model uniquely predicts future system states from past systems states. The behavioral approach is motivated by the aim of obtaining a framework for system analysis that respects the underlying physics and sets up the appropriate mathematical concepts from there.

a. 28-hour day
b. 33 Strategies of War
c. Behavioral model
d. 1990 Clean Air Act

5. _________ and Theory Y are theories of human motivation created and developed by Douglas McGregor at the MIT Sloan School of Management in the 1960s that have been used in human resource management, organizational behavior, organizational communication and organizational development. They describe two very different attitudes toward workforce motivation. McGregor felt that companies followed either one or the other approach.

In _________, which many managers practice, management assumes employees are inherently lazy and will avoid work if they can. They inherently dislike work. Because of this, workers need to be closely supervised and comprehensive systems of controls developed.

a. Management team
b. Cash cow
c. Job enrichment
d. Theory X

6. Theory X and _________ are theories of human motivation created and developed by Douglas McGregor at the MIT Sloan School of Management in the 1960s that have been used in human resource management, organizational behavior, organizational communication and organizational development. They describe two very different attitudes toward workforce motivation. McGregor felt that companies followed either one or the other approach.

In _________, management assumes employees may be ambitious and self-motivated and exercise self-control. It is believed that employees enjoy their mental and physical work duties.

a. Contingency theory
b. Theory Y
c. Design leadership
d. Business Workflow Analysis

7. _________ of the learning curve effect and the closely related experience curve effect express the relationship between equations for experience and efficiency or between efficiency gains and investment in the effort. The experience of 'learning curves' was first observed by the 19th Century German psychologist Hermann Ebbinghaus according to the difficulty of memorizing varying numbers of verbal stimuli, and subsequent learning about the complex processes of learning are discussed in the

.

The rule used for representing the learning curve effect states that the more times a task has been performed, the less time will be required on each subsequent iteration.

a. Point biserial correlation coefficient
b. Models
c. Spatial Decision Support Systems
d. Distribution

8. _________ is a leadership style that defines as leadership that creates voluble and positive change in the followers. A transformational leader focuses on 'transforming' others to help each other, to look out for each other, be encouraging, harmonious, and look out for the organization as a whole. In this leadership, the leader enhances the motivation, moral and performance of his follower group.

a. Strong-Campbell Interest Inventory
b. SESAMO
c. Polynomial conjoint measurement
d. Transformational Leadership

9. There are two types of _________ relationships: formal and informal. Informal relationships develop on their own between partners. Formal _________, on the other hand, refers to assigned relationships, often associated with organizational _________ programs designed to promote employee development or to assist at-risk children and youth.

a. Real Property Administrator
b. Human resource management system
c. Mentoring
d. Fix it twice

10. A _________ is a research instrument consisting of a series of questions and other prompts for the purpose of gathering information from respondents. Although they are often designed for statistical analysis of the responses, this is not always the case. The _________ was invented by Sir Francis Galton.

a. Mystery shoppers
b. Structured interview
c. Questionnaire construction
d. Questionnaire

1. _________ is a subfield of the larger discipline of communication studies. _________, as a field, is the consideration, analysis, and criticism of the role of communication in organizational contexts.

The field traces its lineage through business information, business communication, and early mass communication studies published in the 1930s through the 1950s.

a. Organizational communication
b. AAAI
c. A Stake in the Outcome
d. A4e

2. The term _________ was introduced by anthropologist Edward T. Hall in 1966 to describe set measurable distances between people as they interact. The effects of _________, according to Hall, can be summarized by the following loose rule:

According to Jonathon Tabor distance-spacing theories based on the early animal-like human of German zoologist Heini Hediger, as found in his 1955 book Studies of the Behavior of Captive Animals in Zoos and Circuses. Hediger, in animals, had distinguished between flight distance , critical distance (attack boundary), personal distance (distance separating members of non-contact species, as a pair of swans), and social distance (intraspecies communication distance.)

a. Proxemics
b. 33 Strategies of War
c. 1990 Clean Air Act
d. 28-hour day

3. _________ describes the situation when output from (or information about the result of) an event or phenomenon in the past will influence the same event/phenomenon in the present or future. When an event is part of a chain of cause-and-effect that forms a circuit or loop, then the event is said to 'feed back' into itself.

_________ is also a synonym for:

- _________ signal; the information about the initial event that is the basis for subsequent modification of the event.
- _________ loop; the causal path that leads from the initial generation of the _________ signal to the subsequent modification of the event.

_________ is a mechanism, process or signal that is looped back to control a system within itself. Such a loop is called a _________ loop.

a. Feedback
b. 1990 Clean Air Act
c. Feedback loop
d. Positive feedback

4. _________ is a field of study that looks at how people from differing cultural backgrounds endeavour to communicate.

In years during and preceding the Cold War, the United States economy was largely self-contained because the world was polarized into two separate and competing powers: the east and west. However, changes and advancements in economic relationships, political systems, and technological options began to break down old cultural barriers.

a. 28-hour day
b. 33 Strategies of War
c. 1990 Clean Air Act
d. Cross-cultural communication

5. A _________ is a research instrument consisting of a series of questions and other prompts for the purpose of gathering information from respondents. Although they are often designed for statistical analysis of the responses, this is not always the case. The _________ was invented by Sir Francis Galton.

a. Questionnaire construction
b. Structured interview
c. Mystery shoppers
d. Questionnaire

1. In commerce, _________ is the length of time it takes from a product being conceived until its being available for sale. _________ is important in industries where products are outmoded quickly. A common assumption is that _________ matters most for first-of-a-kind products, but actually the leader often has the luxury of time, while the clock is clearly running for the followers.
   a. Career development
   b. Market entry
   c. Procurement
   d. Time to market

2. A _________ is a volunteer group composed of workers (or even students), usually under the leadership of their supervisor (but they can elect a team leader), who are trained to identify, analyse and solve work-related problems and present their solutions to management in order to improve the performance of the organization, and motivate and enrich the work of employees. When matured, true _________s become self-managing, having gained the confidence of management. _________s are an alternative to the dehumanising concept of the Division of Labour, where workers or individuals are treated like robots.
   a. Connectionist expert systems
   b. Competency-based job descriptions
   c. Certified in Production and Inventory Management
   d. Quality circle

3. _________ is a business management strategy aimed at embedding awareness of quality in all organizational processes. _________ has been widely used in manufacturing, education, hospitals, call centers, government, and service industries, as well as NASA space and science programs.

As defined by the International Organization for Standardization (ISO):

> '_________ is a management approach for an organization, centered on quality, based on the participation of all its members and aiming at long-term success through customer satisfaction, and benefits to all members of the organization and to society.' ISO 8402:1994

One major aim is to reduce variation from every process so that greater consistency of effort is obtained. (Royse, D., Thyer, B., Padgett D., ' Logan T., 2006)

   a. Total quality management
   b. 28-hour day
   c. Quality management
   d. 1990 Clean Air Act

4. _________ is a civil designation for persons who are incorporated in a fixed or permanent way to a society or group: regular member of the working staff, permanent staff distinguished from a supernumerary.

The term '_________' and its counterpart, 'supernumerary,' originated in Spanish and Latin American academy and government; it is now also used in countries all over the world, such as France, the U.S., England, Italy, etc.

There are _________ members of surgical organizations, of universities, of gastronomical associations, etc.

a. Adam Smith
b. Abraham Harold Maslow
c. Affiliation
d. Numerary

5. _________ is a type of thought exhibited by group members who try to minimize conflict and reach consensus without critically testing, analyzing, and evaluating ideas. Individual creativity, uniqueness, and independent thinking are lost in the pursuit of group cohesiveness, as are the advantages of reasonable balance in choice and thought that might normally be obtained by making decisions as a group. During _________, members of the group avoid promoting viewpoints outside the comfort zone of consensus thinking.

a. Groupthink
b. Psychological statistics
c. Self-report inventory
d. Diffusion of responsibility

6. _________ are a class of electronic meeting systems, a collaboration technology designed to support meetings and group work . _________ are distinct from computer supported cooperative work (CSCW) technologies as _________ are more focused on task support, whereas CSCW tools provide general communication support .

_________ were referred to as a Group Support System (GSS) or an electronic meeting system since they shared similar foundations.

a. Learning organization
b. Hoshin Kanri
c. 1990 Clean Air Act
d. Group decision support systems

7. _________ constitute a class of computer-based information systems including knowledge-based systems that support decision-making activities.

_________ are a specific class of computerized information systems that supports business and organizational decision-making activities. A properly-designed _________ is an interactive software-based system intended to help decision makers compile useful information from raw data, documents, personal knowledge, and/or business models to identify and solve problems and make decisions.

a. 28-hour day
b. Decision support systems
c. 1990 Clean Air Act
d. Spatial Decision Support Systems

1. _________ is an idea in the field of Organizational studies and management which describes the psychology, attitudes, experiences, beliefs and Values (personal and cultural values) of an organization. It has been defined as 'the specific collection of values and norms that are shared by people and groups in an organization and that control the way they interact with each other and with stakeholders outside the organization.'

This definition continues to explain organizational values also known as 'beliefs and ideas about what kinds of goals members of an organization should pursue and ideas about the appropriate kinds or standards of behavior organizational members should use to achieve these goals. From organizational values develop organizational norms, guidelines or expectations that prescribe appropriate kinds of behavior by employees in particular situations and control the behavior of organizational members towards one another.'

_________ is not the same as corporate culture.

a. Organizational culture
b. Organizational development
c. Organizational effectiveness
d. Union shop

2. The 'business case for _________', theorizes that in a global marketplace, a company that employs a diverse workforce (both men and women, people of many generations, people from ethnically and racially diverse backgrounds etc.) is better able to understand the demographics of the marketplace it serves and is thus better equipped to thrive in that marketplace than a company that has a more limited range of employee demographics.

An additional corollary suggests that a company that supports the _________ of its workforce can also improve employee satisfaction, productivity and retention.

a. Trademark
b. Virtual team
c. Diversity
d. Kanban

3. The phrase mergers and _________s refers to the aspect of corporate strategy, corporate finance and management dealing with the buying, selling and combining of different companies that can aid, finance, or help a growing company in a given industry grow rapidly without having to create another business entity.

An _________, also known as a takeover or a buyout, is the buying of one company (the 'target') by another. An _________ may be friendly or hostile.

a. AAAI
b. A4e
c. A Stake in the Outcome
d. Acquisition

4. The phrase _________ refers to the aspect of corporate strategy, corporate finance and management dealing with the buying, selling and combining of different companies that can aid, finance, or help a growing company in a given industry grow rapidly without having to create another business entity.

An acquisition, also known as a takeover or a buyout, is the buying of one company (the 'target') by another. An acquisition may be friendly or hostile.

a. 28-hour day
b. Mergers and acquisitions
c. 33 Strategies of War
d. 1990 Clean Air Act

5. In sociology, anthropology and cultural studies, a _________ is a group of people with a culture (whether distinct or hidden) which differentiates them from the larger culture to which they belong. If a particular _________ is characterized by a systematic opposition to the dominant culture, it may be described as a counterculture.

As early as 1950, David Riesman distinguished between a majority, 'which passively accepted commercially provided styles and meanings, and a '_________' which actively sought a minority style ...

a. 1990 Clean Air Act
b. Subculture
c. 33 Strategies of War
d. 28-hour day

6. The _________ is the labour pool in employment. It is generally used to describe those working for a single company or industry, but can also apply to a geographic region like a city, country, state, etc. The term generally excludes the employers or management, and implies those involved in manual labour.
a. Division of labour
b. Pink-collar worker
c. Work-life balance
d. Workforce

7. _________ or _________ data refers to selected population characteristics as used in government, marketing or opinion research, or the _________ profiles used in such research. Note the distinction from the term 'demography' Commonly-used _________s include race, age, income, disabilities, mobility (in terms of travel time to work or number of vehicles available), educational attainment, home ownership, employment status, and even location.

a. Adam Smith
b. Affiliation
c. Abraham Harold Maslow
d. Demographic

8. _________ is a contract between two parties, one being the employer and the other being the employee. An employee may be defined as: 'A person in the service of another under any contract of hire, express or implied, oral or written, where the employer has the power or right to control and direct the employee in the material details of how the work is to be performed.' Black's Law Dictionary page 471 (5th ed. 1979.)

a. Employment
b. Exit interview
c. Employment counsellor
d. Employment rate

9. The term _________ was created by President Lyndon B. Johnson when he signed Executive Order 11246 on September 24, 1965, created to prohibit federal contractors from discriminating against employees on the basis of race, sex, creed, religion, color, or national origin. In more recent times, most employers have also added sexual orientation to the list of non-discrimination.

The Executive Order also required contractors to implement affirmative action plans to increase the participation of minorities and women in the workplace.

a. A4e
b. A Stake in the Outcome
c. AAAI
d. Equal Employment Opportunity

10. _________ is training for the purpose of increasing participants' cultural awareness, knowledge, and skills, which is based on the assumption that the training will benefit an organization by protecting against civil rights violations, increasing the inclusion of different identity groups, and promoting better teamwork.

_________ has been a controversial issue, due to moral considerations as well as questioned efficiency or even counterproductivity.

According to Michael Bird, many project managers may feel that they are treading new territory as they lead project teams made of individuals from different cultures, heterogeneous mixes, and differing demographics.

a. Role conflict
b. Self-disclosure
c. Soft skill
d. Diversity training

Chapter 1

1. d 2. d 3. b

Chapter 2

1. c 2. c 3. d 4. a 5. c 6. c 7. d 8. a 9. d 10. a
11. d 12. d 13. a 14. a 15. d 16. c

Chapter 3

1. b 2. d 3. d 4. a 5. d 6. d 7. c 8. d 9. c 10. a
11. a 12. d 13. b

Chapter 4

1. b 2. d 3. a 4. b 5. d 6. b 7. b 8. d 9. d 10. c
11. d 12. d 13. d 14. d 15. d 16. d 17. a 18. d 19. c 20. d
21. a 22. d 23. d 24. d 25. d

Chapter 5

1. d 2. d 3. b 4. c 5. d 6. d 7. c 8. d 9. d 10. b

Chapter 6

1. d 2. b 3. d 4. d 5. b 6. d 7. d 8. a 9. b

Chapter 7

1. d 2. a 3. d 4. d 5. d 6. b 7. b 8. a 9. d 10. b
11. a 12. c 13. d 14. d 15. d 16. d 17. b

Chapter 8

1. d 2. d 3. d 4. d 5. d 6. d 7. d 8. a 9. c

Chapter 9

1. b 2. d 3. c 4. d 5. a 6. d 7. d 8. c

Chapter 10

1. a 2. d 3. a 4. d 5. d 6. d 7. a 8. d 9. b 10. d
11. c 12. c 13. b 14. d 15. a 16. a 17. b 18. d 19. a 20. d
21. d 22. b 23. d 24. d 25. d 26. d 27. d 28. d

Chapter 11

1. d 2. d 3. d 4. c 5. d 6. c 7. d 8. c 9. a

Chapter 12

1. c 2. d 3. c 4. b 5. b 6. a 7. a 8. d 9. d 10. d
11. a 12. d 13. a 14. a

Chapter 13

1. a	2. d	3. d	4. d	5. a	6. d	7. b	8. c	9. c	10. b
11. d	12. d	13. a	14. d	15. d	16. d	17. d	18. b	19. d	20. d
21. c	22. d	23. d	24. b	25. d	26. d	27. a	28. d	29. c	30. d

Chapter 14

1. d	2. c	3. b	4. c	5. d	6. d	7. a	8. b	9. d	10. b
11. d	12. d	13. c	14. d	15. b					

Chapter 15

1. c	2. d	3. d	4. c	5. d	6. b	7. b	8. d	9. c	10. d

Chapter 16

1. a	2. a	3. a	4. d	5. d

Chapter 17

1. d	2. d	3. a	4. d	5. a	6. d	7. b

Chapter 18

1. a	2. c	3. d	4. b	5. b	6. d	7. d	8. a	9. d	10. d

www.ingramcontent.com/pod-product-compliance
Lightning Source LLC
Chambersburg PA
CBHW081219230426
43666CB00015B/2795